CRITICAL PRAISE FOR

BIG SUGAR

Winner of the Robert F. Kennedy Book Award

"A beautiful book about an ugly industry...A skillful, evocative delineation of [the] culture that grows up around sugar agriculture: the growers, the cutters, the drivers, the peddlers, the shopkeepers, the whores, the children...Wilkinson observes the [cutters] and their surroundings with the detail of a video camera, and he writes about them like an angel."
—*New York Newsday*

"The book [Wilkinson] has written not only evokes the life of the workers with marvelous compassion and understated outrage but for the first time tells the truth about what is probably one of the harshest, most labor intensive and tyrannical industries in the United States....[Wilkinson's] is the America just out of sight from the highway, a place in which interest and indifference connive to permit the intolerable to persist."
—*Los Angeles Times*

"A disturbing book about the hard, ugly life of sugar cane cutters in South Florida...Never before perhaps has a writer put into print their plight so skillfully....Wilkinson is an author with a wondrous eye, a tape-recorder sort of authenticity, and an amazing clarity of prose....He pounds the reader with information...and it is heavy stuff, beautifully reported."

—*Washington Post Book World*

"A rare piece of work...A book you can walk into and smell the plants and hear the people talk...A handsome, spare, and truthful account...like so much of the best journalism, it is cheerful at heart and a strong antidote to dishonesty, silliness, and gloom."

—Garrison Keillor

"Sharp...vivid...Mr. Wilkinson's shrewd eye and sympathetic ear [have] managed to penetrate the mystery and the misery."

—*The New York Times Book Review*

"A tautly written exposé...The Jamaican [cane] cutters, like other migrant workers, do work that is too hard, dirty and low-paying for the natives of the rich countries. With skill and compassion, Wilkinson has shown us their faces and let us hear their voices."

—*Chicago Tribune*

BIG SUGAR

ALSO BY ALEC WILKINSON

MIDNIGHTS: *A Year with the Wellfleet Police* (1982)

MOONSHINE: *A Life in Pursuit of White Liquor* (1985)

ALEC WILKINSON

BIG SUGAR

Seasons in the Cane Fields of Florida

VINTAGE BOOKS
A DIVISION OF RANDOM HOUSE, INC.
NEW YORK

FIRST VINTAGE BOOKS EDITION, NOVEMBER 1990

 Published in the United States by Vintage Books, a division of Random House, Inc., New York, and simultaneously in Canada by Random House of Canada Limited, Toronto. Originally published in hardcover by Alfred A. Knopf, Inc., in 1989.

Portions of this work were originally published in *The New Yorker.*

Library of Congress Cataloging-in-Publication Data
Wilkinson, Alec, 1952-
Big sugar : seasons in the cane fields of Florida / Alec Wilkinson. — 1st Vintage Books ed.
p. cm.
ISBN 0-679-73187-3
1. Sugar workers—Florida. 2. Migrant agricultural laborers—Florida. 3. Alien labor—Florida. I. Title.
[HD8039.S86U67 1990]
331.5'44—dc20 90-50164
CIP

Manufactured in the United States of America
10 9 8 7 6 5 4 3 2 1

For

Sara Barrett

BIG SUGAR

1

The most perilous work in America is the harvest by hand of sugar cane in south Florida. It is performed by men from the West Indies who live in barracks on the sugar plantations. The majority come from Jamaica, but they also come from Barbados, St. Vincent, St. Lucia, and Dominica. The white people call them offshore workers, or offshores, or H-2 workers (after the government program overseeing their use), or H-2's, or hand-cutters, or cutters, or, simply, and most often, Jamaicans. As a rule they are tall and long-limbed. They walk like dancers, and they have a taut, steely look to their arms and backs and shoulders and legs, as if they were made from wires and pulleys, as if they were designed for the task. The harvest begins in the fall and ends in the spring. Ten thousand cutters take part; they constitute the largest group of foreign workers admitted each year to this country. Often they spend as much time abroad as at home. Their quarters are cheerless and without any privacy, the food they are served is not to their liking, they are frequently cheated by their employers, and they are constantly tormented by loneliness and by anxiety over the lives their wives and girlfriends and families and friends are living without them at home. In the fields they wear aluminum guards on their hands, their shins, and their knees, as well as heavy boots on their feet. Even so, more than one in every three of them cuts himself or is cut by someone who has lost control of his knife, or wrenches his back, or suffers an attack of some kind in the heat, or steps in a rabbit hole and turns an ankle, or is bitten by fire ants, or pierces his eye or his eardrum with a sharp leaf of cane while bending over and grabbing a stalk. If the last is the case and you ask him what happened, he is likely to say, "I spear up in a cane top."

Sugar cane is grown on the south shore of Lake Okeechobee, the body of water depicted on the Florida license plate. A singular quality of the area's soil—it is unusually soft—makes harvesting the crop by machine problematic; mechanical harvesters often bog and tear up the fields and pull the cane from the soil by the roots. Sugar cane returns each year from previous plantings, like grass—a field usually supplies five crops before being replanted—so it is important that the roots not be damaged. Approximately a quarter of the crop is harvested mechanically. Machines are used mainly in fields where the soil is more substantial. In addition to being dangerous, cutting sugar cane is monotonous and fatiguing. It is stoop labor. The cutters perform the bulk of their task bent over at the waist; to stand upright they frequently brace themselves with one hand on their backs and rise slowly.

What they are paid is determined by means of a piece rate calculated on the assumption that each will account for at least a ton of sugar cane an hour. The growers assign a price, called a row price, to a cut row of cane, a cut row being two side-by-side rows. Rows are either one quarter mile or one half mile long, depending on the dimensions of the field. Because of the danger and the tedium and the piece rate, Americans have shunned work in cane. A cutter has said that an American once told him, "If sugar cane ever grew at my door, I would find another door to go out of." In the annals of Florida agriculture, the profitable cultivation of sugar cane is a recent event; it was first grown with significant commercial success in 1931 by the United States Sugar Corporation. For the next eleven years the crop was harvested by black men recruited throughout the South. White men would travel on behalf of the corporation to cities like Memphis or Tuscaloosa and walk through the black part of town offering free transportation and medical care and housing and meals to anyone who would cut sugar cane in Florida, and when the men arrived they would hear that they owed the corporation for the ride and for the equipment to cut cane and that they couldn't leave the plantation until they had satisfied their debts. To find sufficient sources of labor, representatives of the corporation had to keep traveling farther from south Florida, to reach places where word of their practices had not yet arrived. During the early nineteen-forties they began to find that men who might otherwise have cut sugar cane had moved north to jobs at factories or else were abroad at the war. West Indians have cut the sugar cane crop in south Florida for more than forty-five years. They appeared in the fields in the fall of 1943, the year after the United States Sugar Corporation, which then held eighty-six per cent of the acreage, was indicted by a federal grand jury in Tampa for carrying out a conspiracy to commit slavery.

Sugar cane is grown also in Texas, Louisiana, Hawaii, and Puerto Rico. As well as being the only one that is harvested by hand, Florida's crop is by far the largest, accounting for more than forty per cent of all the sugar cane grown in America. There are plantings of significance in Martin and Glades counties, but most of the acreage, as well as all seven of the mills, lies within Hendry and Palm Beach counties, in fields outside the towns of Pahokee, Belle Glade, South Bay, Clewiston, and Moore Haven. Those first to be planted were the fields outside Clewiston, the home of U.S. Sugar.

The way the West Indians pronounce Clewiston suggests a place cooled by breezes from the sea. (It is not.) It is a small, lonesome, dreary, and prosperous company town, sixty miles west of Palm Beach. It has seven thousand inhabitants. It was built in the late nineteen-twenties according to plans drawn up in Boston by a firm working for the Southern Sugar Corporation, which wanted a showcase town for its headquarters (Southern Sugar went bankrupt in 1930; its assets were taken over by U.S. Sugar). A promotional booklet, published in 1941 by U.S. Sugar, describes Clewiston as "one of the few custom, or tailor-made cities, developed along preconceived plans." From above, the design of the town resembles two narrow tombstones laid side by side, heads against the lake. The streets run mainly on the grid; by the lake, a few describe arcs. One way to think of Clewiston is as an interruption of the cane. Route 27 leaves the fields and passes through the center of town, is the main street, and is called the Sugarland Highway. It has five stoplights. The streetlamps along it line up as straight as the lights on a runway. At one end of town is a sign saying "Welcome to Clewiston, America's Sweetest Town." At the other is a stand of bamboo beside a canal leading into the lake. Big, haughty, stick-legged herons roost in the bamboo trees like figures on a Chinese scroll.

The most prominent building in town is the mill, called the Sugar House, which begins running in the fall and runs around the clock until spring. The majority of the town's black population live beside the mill in a neighborhood called Harlem. Sometimes white men driving beat-up old cars and holding beer cans pull up to one of the men standing on Main Street outside the Down Beat Super Disco, or Perry's Records, or Whitfield's Child Care Center, or the 24 Hour Thang, or Betty's New Suite Inn, or Another World Club, or Sonny's Service Center, or the Elbert Barber Shop, or Elbert's Used Cars ("We Finance, Buy Here") and roll down their window and say, "Know where I can get some pussy?" The tallest buildings in Harlem are the churches—the Church of God, the Tabernacle of Witness Deliverance, and the Greater Friendship Missionary Baptist Church. In the evening the streets are full of children. Many have West Indian blood and are exceptionally handsome. The people of Harlem live with the constant sound of the mill. The houses closest to it lie just across a canal from the company land. Periodically, when conditions are right at the mill, and the wind is blowing from the east, the mill disperses over Harlem a stench like that of raw sewage.

There is nowhere in Clewiston from which a person cannot arrive, after a few minutes' walk, in the cane fields. The fields lie on three sides of the town, the lake on the fourth. From the top of the levee the fields have the broad, uniform, slightly-swaying-in-the-wind look of a prairie. Sugar cane is a cast-iron crop: it survives episodes of freezing and flooding; it survives fire; in Florida it has few pests and few diseases; its water supply, based on a series of canals fed by the lake, is all but invulnerable to drought; and its value is protected by arrangements with the government, so that fields of it have the pleasing, stable look of a sound investment; they look like money in the bank. The fields run straight to the horizon. Sugar cane is a row crop, and the arrangement over so many miles of rows and grids and blocks gives the fields an appearance as orderly and patterned and precise as a design on a piece of fabric. A person riding in a car on the highway or on one of the paved roads winding through the fields, both of which lie on beds built up from the soil, looks out his window across vistas that are wide and deep and as flat as a body of water. The aisles of cane revolve as he passes, like merchandise on display. The sky falls to the horizon like a curtain; the fields of cane, the taller woods beyond, and the sky, foreshortened by the eye, appear to lie on top of each other like layers of geology. The fields absorb the heat of the sun and send it back toward the sky in shimmers. For the most part the fields are without variation, so that any change—a cypress head, the stacks of a mill, a silo for cattle feed—looms like a destination. The skies are so large that several kinds of weather sometimes take place in them at once.

Across all this distance a person occasionally sees a small flash of light, like someone sending a signal with a mirror, like a distress call, like a little chip of mica catching the light, and that is the sun striking the blade of the cane knife as the cutter raises it above his shoulder and brings it down towards the field. If the person were moved to establish the source of the light and went closer to the field, he would begin to discern the colors of the cutters' clothes, then the human form; closer still, he would begin to hear the faint, thudding sound of the blade; closer still, then, the voice of the pusher, the man who oversees the cutters at work: "Watch them leaves, cut the top them off, pile that cane good, I ain't joking now."

I went to Clewiston for the first time in 1984, because it had appeared as the dateline on a newspaper article I had read about the sugar business, and over the next four years I kept going back. Most of the time I stayed on Royal Palm Way at the Clewiston Inn, which, I learned, is owned by U.S. Sugar. At the front desk they sell windbreakers and polo shirts bearing the company logo. When there were no rooms—when the Inn was expecting a delegation to the industry from Washington which had booked the whole place, or when there was a bass-fishing tournament going on at the lake—I stayed in one of the cement-block motels along the highway, where the car and truck headlights penetrated the curtains and threw shadows all night on the walls and the ceiling, where I was the only person without a boat on a trailer parked outside my door, and where when I got up in the morning my car was the only one left in the lot. At night I would have a steak and two beers at Tony's Glades Restaurant, and drive out to the camp at Moore Haven to look at the cutters from the highway. Or I went to Donnelly's at the east end of town, where the light was better and I could read if I wanted to. Saturday nights at Donnelly's I became accustomed to the sight of big fat men who wore their bellies like physical memories of other nights when they had come into some town hauling a bass boat and had launched it at dawn at the marina and fished all day and then gone into a restaurant and ordered highballs and raised their glasses to each other and their sunburned faces and said, "Here's to a great weekend!" then, worn out from the day on the water, had eaten in silence, except maybe to ask, "How's your steak, buddy; I got a great piece of meat!" the blue edge of a tattoo just showing beneath the hem of the sleeve of their T-shirt. One night in Donnelly's I saw the best-looking woman I had seen in my years in Clewiston sitting by herself at a table and reading the local paper and finally one man at a table nearby finished his steak and turned to her and said, "So what's new today?" and she looked up from the paper and said, "Went hog hunting," and he nodded and she went back to reading. There were always lots of silences. One night I sat next to a family having dinner, and I heard the oldest child, a teenage girl, tell her parents, "If you think I'm spending the rest of my life in Clewiston, you've been dreaming too much."

While I was in Clewiston, the Lakeport Volunteer Firemen held a pancake breakfast; Sheriff Dyess cut the ribbon on the new Hendry County Jail in Labelle (several of the town's prominent citizens sat as prisoners in the cells while townspeople toured the facilities); Hatfield's Mobile Home Sales advertised a 1986 Fleetwood double-wide (three bedrooms, two bathrooms, large living room, large den), furnished (including ceiling fans), and set up on a lot for $222.23 a month; "In Our Opinion . . .," a column in the Clewiston *News*, asked, "What do you want Santa Claus to bring you for Christmas?" to which one woman answered, "A washing machine, cause mine tore up."; two men penning cows near a cabbage hammock on the Brighton Seminole Indian Reservation discovered a crashed plane; the Tommy Smith family (Tommy, June, and Scott) were chosen Hendry County Farm Family of the Year; a sixteen-year-old boy watched his mother and father struggle over control of a semiautomatic pistol (when they broke apart, the gun fired and his mother was killed); "Christmas in Paris," the United Methodist Women's bazaar, featured "French related items" and a robot that wished people Merry Christmas; the Association for Retarded Citizens held a car wash; a McDonald's opened; the Clewiston police asked the public's help in locating Audie Lee Hopkins, twenty-four years old, a heavy-equipment operator with brown hair to his shoulders, green eyes, a skull and "Lee" tattooed on his left forearm, last seen driving a white 1975 two-door Ford; Sandra Holder hung "Impressions by Sandra" at the Clewiston National Bank (among the works, *Kief*, a portrait of an Arabian horse); *Jesus Is Lord*, a play about the Crucifixion, had a run of six days at the John Boy Auditorium; Joni Busbee was crowned Miss Hendry County at the Hendry County Fair and Livestock Show (theme: "Honoring Hendry County's Harvest"; attendance: nineteen thousand four hundred thirty-three, second most ever; during the talent portion of the competition, Miss Busbee performed the monologue "A Phone Call from the Lord"); on the Big Cypress Reservation, members of the Seminole Tribal Housing Authority cut the ribbon on their new office; a hunter fell from a deer stand and died; a tornado derailed eight empty cane cars and pushed twenty-eight cars approximately half a mile east; the Greater Friendship Baptist Church turned fifty-nine and together with the Clewiston Pentecostal Holiness Church held a revival with Reverend Billy Thompson in a big tent out by the highway; the Hendry County Sheriff's Department offered "Women's Firearm Training and Safety"; the Florida Department of Plant Industry announced it was selling Fire Ant Bait; a man was arrested for trespassing fenced pasture; the football team went to the quarterfinals of the state championship (the week before the game, the cheerleaders painted "Tigers Are #1" in blue and yellow on the windows of the stores along the Sugarland Highway; late Saturday afternoon, they washed them off); letters in the *News* appeared under the headlines "America's Safest Town," "Head Lice Concern," "Minister Says Merchants Can Define Pornography," and "Tax Peeves Citizen."

2

The cutters live in camps maintained by the growers. Some are near towns (one is in Belle Glade), and some are in the fields. A few are beside the mills. Some are surrounded by chain-link fences, a number have checkpoints, and all are off limits to outsiders.

At the smallest camps live perhaps a hundred and fifty cutters, at the largest two thousand. How many are permitted to live in a barracks is determined by a government regulation concerning the minimum space to which a cutter is entitled.

Among the twenty-one camps are approximately equal numbers of two kinds: villages consisting of one-room cottages, and larger buildings which hold numbers of cutters. The villages are the older design. They were built on sites chosen for being central among the fields their cutters were to harvest. Each camp was responsible for three to four thousand acres. In times past the villages often included a chapel, a commissary, and occasionally a school. Perhaps half of the men who worked on the harvest lived year-round in the camps and had families. The men planted cane and cultivated the fields and kept up the farm roads and ditches. Most of the cottages are made of cement and finished with stucco. They have cement floors that can be washed out with garden hoses. Some are of Homosote and sit on stilts. Most have porches by the front door and a sink in which the cutters wash their clothes and the sap from their knives.

The majority of the larger barracks are built of cement from the simplest plans. They are flat roofed and have two or three stories; they look like shoeboxes. Usually they are painted tan. A number are in disrepair. Some look like slums. Often there is trash in the yard. Occasionally it is raked into piles and set on fire. Dogs and chickens scavenge the ashes. Shade is unusual. The roofs take the full heat of the sky. The floors are divided into large open rooms. Within them the air is still. Heat collects. No provisions have been made for relieving the heat or for moving the air. In town the cutters buy fans that run on batteries and place them beside their beds. Sanitation is lax. The cutters sometimes question the purity of the water. Stalls in the bathrooms have no doors. There is noise and smoke. The buildings have been allowed to dilapidate. On their own against the landscape they appear stolid and dismal and formal and severe, like a place a person might end up only by means of bad luck. They look like something you would expect to see out near the airport in a country with a tropical climate and a faltering currency. The Jamaicans think the buildings look like big boats moored in the fields. At night, with their rows of windows white against the darkness, they have the slightly metallic, incandescent look of a liner. All lack the meanest embellishment.

The cutters sleep in double-decker bunk beds lined in rows, heads to the walls, with an aisle down the middle of the room. Between each bed is room enough for a man to stand and pull on his pants. Each bed has a gray wool blanket. The cutters are given sheets, which are exchanged every two weeks. The cutters prefer the lower bunks. You can drape a sheet or a towel from the top like a curtain and have privacy and also block out some of the light, which is from the ceiling and harsh. Plus, the heat rises and so do the smells. Lying in bed at night the cutters can feel the heat settling on them. In some camps lockers stand between the beds. At others they are set at the ends of the room. The men play cards across the beds, or checkers; they draw checkerboards on the sides of cardboard boxes and use bottle caps for pieces. At the head of many of the top bunks are windows. As the darkness fills them the windows turn shiny and reflective and eventually what the cutters see as they lie there looking out at the fields are their own faces staring back at them.

Some of the bunks are empty, vacated by cutters who have slipped the contract. In a prosperous year the empty beds are piled with suitcases the cutters buy in town and fill with women's dresses and children's clothes and paper towels and cans of cocktail nuts to take back to the islands. In a bad year, what the cutters call bossman's year, the beds just stay empty.

A few camps have washing machines. Most only have sinks. To clean their work clothes the cutters pour powdered detergent on them and scrub them, as if they were washing their clothes in a river. Some camps have dryers. If there is no clothesline in the yard, the cutters weave the sleeves of their shirts through the links of the fences or wrap them around the railings of the balconies. Flapping in the wind, the shirts and trousers look festive. They give the camp a carnival air. They make it look as if the buildings were put up for some other purpose and have been abandoned and taken over by squatters. At camps without fences or balconies, cutters string up clotheslines inside the barracks. Whether they wash their clothes on any given day has to do with how tired they are when they return from the fields. If they haven't got the energy to wash them, they hang their clothes anyway on the lines to dry. This disheartens the camp generally because of the smell and because it forces the cutters to live constantly among the dirt of the fields. It gets into their beds and their hair and their stores of food.

From the water pipes above the beds the cutters hang the dress clothes they arrived in. Men who have had the experience of a season know to bring extra clothes so they can date. They cannot easily get their clothes to the cleaners; towards the end of the season, in dressing for town, the cutters freshen up their shirts by spraying them with deodorant.

A cutter will come in from the fields and remove his shirt and sit in a chair and not move. You note his presence. You leave. You return. He has remained where he was without moving. Or one might lie on the bed and throw his arm over his eyes to keep out the light and fall asleep immediately. (Often you see a man asleep with his head beside a tape player turned up loud, or by a television screen, the blue light playing across his face.) Or sit and unwrap the bindings he wears to brace his wrist so slowly that he reminds you of a man removing bandages from a wound. Sometimes a cutter you know looks at you out of eyes that show the effort of trying to think who you are, of returning from where he is in his mind to greet you. As you pass among the rows of bunks, the cutters observe you with eyes that look like the eyes of men who are fighting a disease.

The camps in the country are out among the fields and remote from any amusement. At night the cutters who have revived can stand in the darkness and look out at the glows thrown up on the horizon by the distant towns. They call the West Indies from the pay phones in the yards. They wander out among the fields. They fish in the canals; the water reflects the lights of the camp so it looks as if the surface has been varnished or lacquered or polished to a shine. They play coon cane, peter pot, rummy, and poker. They sit at card tables under signs that say "Gambling Will Not Be Permitted At Any Time" and raise their hands above their heads and slap down dominoes with such force that the tables shake. They sit on the edge of their beds and listen to a preacher on the radio tell them their lives are steeped in sin and that mansions await them in heaven or watch professional wrestling or a martial-arts movie or go off to a corner so as not to disturb the others and file the blades of their knives or shave the handles to fit their palms. They receive peddlers. Women visit. They bring a blanket and roll it out at the edge of the fields. Or work in their cars. The men ask the rate and how much time they will have, and the women tell them, "As long as it stay."

They cook on hot plates they are permitted to have only for making coffee and tea. To conceal the hot plates they put them in cardboard boxes by the side of their beds and cover the pots with the flaps of the box and make soup or fry fish. Steam rises from the boxes, misting the windows. When a number of men are cooking, it is sometimes not possible to see through the smoke and the steam from one end of a barracks to the other. What they make mostly is soup with thick dumplings called spinners. At one camp a cook in the past planted cassava beside one of the barracks; the cutters go out and collect it and add it to their soups. The mess halls serve cornmeal, porridge, or oatmeal, or farina and eggs and bacon and toast and tea and coffee for breakfast, and fried fish, or chili beef, or macaroni, or goat curry, or fried chicken, baked beans, and potatoes for dinner, according to the day. In the fields the cutters get braised oxtails, or pig's feet, or beef stew, as well as rice and red beans, and maybe turnip greens or mustard greens. The food is not even close to their liking. They feel it hasn't got the ingredients to give them strength. It is too starchy and bland and greasy a diet for a man who spends all day laboring in a cane field.

To supplement the food they are served the cutters make a drink from a base of egg nog, sugar, and Guinness Stout. To it they add some combination of carrot juice, milk, V-8, nutmeg, a beaten egg, evaporated milk, or Nutrament. Jamaicans call this drink petrol; Barbadians call it shandy. Sometimes Barbadians leave out the egg nog. Grocery stores in Clewiston and Belle Glade and Pahokee sell the ingredients in displays set up for the cutters. To the storeowners the cutters are walking dollar signs; they raise their prices for the season. Many cutters feel it takes too long to eat the meal they are served in the fields; they fear that in the time they are away from their rows the work will be assigned to somebody else. Instead, they fill the drink jugs they are given with petrol and bring them to the fields for lunch. In the evening they drink large glasses of petrol with the meals they make for themselves; some men like then to add a little brandy to the mixture. A popular Jamaican recipe for strong petrol is carrot juice, sugar, evaporated milk, Nutrament, two bottles of stout, and one carton of egg nog. Petrol gives you strength to cut cane, the cutters say, and more power for your holiday.

Most cutters prefer the larger camps, even though the food and the pay are not as good as at the smaller camps, and there are also the aggravations of heat and lack of cleanliness and crowding. They like the larger camps because there is more activity. The camp in Belle Glade is close to a number of bars. The problem living there is getting enough sleep to be fit for work in the morning. The cutters are in and out of the bars all night, spending their money and drinking beer and dancing. Since they are handsome, they are popular with the local women, who like their accents. The bars are small and dark as caves. It is hard to make out faces. Mainly the bars feature reggae. Conversation is impossible. You go out the swinging screen door of the barracks and down the stairs and turn left on the street and walk to the end of the block and you are in the pleasure district of Belle Glade.

3

A peculiarity of the harvest is the burning of the fields the day before cutting. The fires are spectacular. They consume the leaves and tops, which slow down the cutters and clog the mill, and they clear the fields of wildlife. They take place late in the morning or early in the afternoon. As your eyes circle the horizon you can often find more than one. In the distance they look like disasters, like air strikes, like war. White smoke means the field is damp and burning poorly. Black is ideal. The dark, rising columns put the fields in shadow. What light filters through is unnatural, like the light before a storm, except that it is not green, it is orange, or amber, like the light from a stoplight; it makes a person look as if he is blushing. The fires make a furnace of the fields. Currents of heat spin like whirlpools in the air above the flames. At a certain proximity you can feel the heat through the closed windows of a car. In the vicinity of the burn the air smells like roasted corn (sugar cane and corn are related). Occasionally you can detect it on the wind in town. Sometimes you see an ash from the fields drifting in the air before you on Main Street. The fires make a terrific amount of noise. A man I know who woke as a child to the bombing of Pearl Harbor went back to sleep thinking: *It is only the burning of the cane fields.* On the hottest burns there is a thick oily look to the smoke and the flames. The egrets fly in and out of the fires, rising and falling on the hot, churning air.

Prudent burners take several precautions. Burning one of two bordering fields, they wet the edge of one or the other, usually the one being burned, to prevent the flames from jumping. Or run a tractor down two or three rows at the border and burn them against the wind, creating a firebreak. Down any rows beneath power lines or near houses they also run tractors, to keep the flames low to the ground. Some growers send a tractor down the outside row of any field they burn in order to make a path for the man lighting the fire and for the water wagon. This cuts the profit of the field, not only for the money spent on the tractor and driver, but also because fallen cane is more expensive to harvest, so many growers don't bother.

There are two methods of burning: hot and cold—with the wind, that is, or against it. On a cold burn the fire stays closer to the ground and is easier to manage. The flames take longer to cross the field and leave the tops of the stalks intact, but a burner is less likely to have someone trapped in the field or lose control of his fire. If the cane is damp, or the burner wants to hurry up his burn, or wants a fire that clears out as much trash as possible, he burns hot. What he gets is a horse race of flame across the fields. As fast as the wind will carry the fire, he can burn a hundred acres. A hundred acres burned cold might take two hours; the fire creeps against the wind. Early in the season, when the cane is green and the fires less vigorous, growers mostly burn hot. Later, when the cane is dry, they burn cold, especially after a freeze. After a freeze the fields burn as if gasoline has been sprayed on them. What people say is that after a freeze the fields explode.

Cold burning is also called back burning. Flyers, burning leaves that drift into other fields and set them on fire, are more likely to occur in back-burned fields; the slow-moving flames ignite not only the cane but also the palmettos and cabbage palms that border the fields; their fibrous leaves, slow to catch, burn stubbornly; borne on the wind, they can set ablaze fields a mile away. On days of high wind, burners stand on the roofs of their trucks and scan the far fields for smoke. After a freeze the fires sometimes jump the canals, because the weeds on the surface of the canals are dry. If a burner loses control of a fire (happens, rarely), he calls the Forest Service. A deft burner walks the fire across the field as easily as if he had it on a leash.

Burners light two or three sides of a field, depending on the direction and force of the wind. Lighting three sides helps move the flame in low wind. The fire draws straight up and burns stronger. The trickiest burns, the finesse burns, are those involving fields surrounded by another man's holdings. In order to collect his cane, a grower sends two men into the wind, lighting all four sides, and the flames meet in the center of the field. Some burners ignite all four sides as common practice, but most leave at least one side open for the snakes and rats and rabbits and raccoons and pigs to escape. If the field being burned is one beside others, the animals disappear into the bordering field, often without being seen. If the burn involves the last block of a field, they hotfoot it across the open ground to cover. In their terror to find shelter they sometimes run straight at a person, almost arriving before recovering their senses. Sometimes, spooked, they run back into the field. Some field bosses keep rifles in their pickups to put out of their misery animals run over by the flames.

The pace of many fires is irregular. If rain has fallen the night before, a field is not burned until the afternoon; if there has been no particular wind or if the day has not been sunny or dry, the fire will pause here and there and be spiritless. Lightning sometimes ignites patches of cane, which the rain puts out. These places never return; the fire stutters when it hits them. A field burned early in the morning following the dew, or after a rain, may burn well on the edges, where the wind and sun have reached it, but not inside. The fire will start fast, creep across the middle, then bolt in reaching the drier cane at the opposite end. Shifts of wind slow a fire.

To make the green fields burn more thoroughly early in the season, growers spray them with paraquat, which causes the leaves to wither. Fields that have been back burned or have not been paraquated or have not frozen sometimes don't look very different from a field that hasn't been burned. A person looking closely will notice he can see between the rows, that the leaves lower on the stalks are gone, and that the stalks are scorched, but the green tops and flowers will still be in place. A perfectly burned field would contain only stalks.

Sometimes a well-burned field hardly looks burned at all. The edges of a field never burn as completely as the interior, no matter how it is burned or when (the fire has not picked up enough force at the start, or has broken by the end), so it is not easy to tell how completely a field has burned from outside it. A field is never burned twice. There is nothing left really to catch fire; also the delay of the harvest and the second fire would cause a loss of sugar. Mills accept cane up to seven days after it has burned but prefer it right away. After three days the sugar becomes more difficult to extract.

If you are standing at the edge of a burning field, the flame roars up then breaks like a wave as it reaches you. People who have driven through the fires, or close along the edge of a field that is burning, say that the flames hit the hood of the car and splash off it like water.

Conditions for burning are only infrequently ideal. Because the land is so flat, the wind blows from all points of the compass and can wheel in a circle quickly. On days of varying wind, burning is tricky. At a moment of unpredictable wind a careful burner might walk a few yards into the corner of a field and light it to see what will happen. Some people say that the worst time to burn is in a time of dead wind, because the fire creates its own draw and goes where it wants to. Before lighting a fire, a burner checks the wind, checks the path he has to walk, notes any power lines, checks the position of his water wagon, the grass on the headland to see if there are places where the fire might jump, and any other places where it might get away from him. When they are in a hurry some burners light fires under the power lines without precautions, figuring the power lines can take it.

The water wagons are drawn by tractors and hold a thousand gallons. On the top is a hatch through which a man can climb if he has to. You'd think it would be like jumping into a teakettle on a stove, but the fire passes quickly. If a burner is trapped near a ditch bank, he dives into the canal and stays as much under water as he can until the flame passes. The tractors are not fast enough to outrun a fire and sometimes a man pulling the water wagon can get caught and the only thing to do is drive to the far corner of the field and spray down the field around him. Now and then a fire overtakes a tractor or a pickup truck trapped in a field. The machine still works after, but it sure dulls the finish.

Some of the bigger growers have burn crews, men who perform other tasks on the farm but are available to carry a firepot and know what to do with it. Smaller ones often use anyone handy. When the tractor drivers see their supervisor's truck approaching, they strive to appear deeply engaged in their work. If he happens to arrive at a moment when a crew is idle, a kind of musical-chairs-like activity takes place around the machines, because the drivers know he is looking for someone to send down a cane row on a sweltering day with a burn pot, dodging snakes. When you see a man in the distance walking down a ditch bank lighting a cane row, and then you see him drop the firepot, or turn it away from the cane field and point it at the ground, and start doing a little dance, you are looking at a man who has found a snake. Few people like to carry the firepot. Over the quarter- or half-mile length of the row it grows heavy. Unless the row has been run down by a tractor, one is fighting one's way against the cane. The heat can be fearsome. Not only is finding a snake unsettling, but the entire time a burner is messing with the snake, he can hear the fire gaining behind him.

Burners carry Forest Service firepots. They look like oiling cans with a wick at the end of the nozzle. Fuel drips past the lit wick and is ignited and drops onto the cane. The mixture in the pots is half gas, half diesel; diesel on its own wouldn't light and gas would explode. Burners carry the pots in the beds of their trucks and light them with matches or cigarette lighters. There is a technique to carrying the pot. If a person holds the pot pointed down at too great an angle, it will leak and he will find the pot in flames from the fuel dripping over it. Also, holding the pot at too steep an angle is wasteful of fuel. A good burner can burn sixty acres with half a pot or two fields with one pot. Sometimes the burn pots develop cracks in their gaskets and leak and catch fire and the only thing to do is toss them into the canal; the hotter the pot gets, the more the gasket expands, the more fuel escapes.

No one in south Florida knows how burning began. It is generally believed that lightning struck a field, or someone dropped a cigarette. After the grower put out the fire, he harvested the cane anyway. The harvesting went faster, and when he got the cane to the mill he discovered he had not lost much sugar. It is possible that burning started somewhere else and word of the practice traveled to Florida. It began there during the nineteen-forties. At first it was done only when growers were short on labor. In most places cane is burned before harvest. In some places where it is harvested by machine (Louisiana, for example) the cane is cut first, then laid on the ground and set on fire. In order to have more choice on when to harvest, Australians cut the cane green. Cutters there are subject to something called Wheal's Disease, which is spread by rats who chew on the cane and infects the cutters through scratches on their hands made by the cane leaves and stalks. Burning controls it.

Until the nineteen-sixties growers burned at night. Fires were less difficult to control because the dew had fallen (but not saturated the fields), and the wind was low. In addition, it was easier to keep track of the fire's progress, especially when it reached the edges of the field; a burn crew could look for flame in the darkness, whereas during the day they have to watch for smoke. People on the coasts complained that smoke from burns made at night stayed close to the ground and drifted their way. During the day, smoke rose and dispersed. In order to burn now at night a grower needs a permit from the Forest Service, which refuses most requests. A grower with a particularly difficult burn—a field near houses, or one among others he intends to harvest later—might apply for a night burn.

As a rule, there is no burning before nine in the morning, and all burns must be out by an hour before sunset. Except following a frost, there is generally no burning early in the morning anyway, because of the dew. How much cane a grower burns depends on the mill's request and the weather. Growers try to stay about a day-and-a-half's loading ahead on their burns. The most likely reason for an early morning burn would be that a grower was trying to make up time lost somewhere on repairs to machinery, or a breakdown at the mill, or a labor problem, or to rain. The growers are in a constant dance with the weather. The trickiest scheduling of burns is on days of intermittent rain. A grower wants time for the wind to dry his fields, but he doesn't want to lose his chance to the next arrival of rain. For a person harvesting mechanically a poor burn means more trash delivered to the mill and less money for his cane. For a grower harvesting by hand it means paying more for his harvest or risking strife with the labor. A slack fire is always a disappointment.

Birds are drawn in flocks to the flames. They arrive in hysterics. Borne on the currents of heat, grasshoppers shoot like rockets from the fields. The birds read the vectors of their flight and pick them cleanly from the air. Grackles and rice birds show up in numbers, but most of the birds are egrets. They hug the flames; they disappear into them; they settle on the fields and walk right up to the fires, as if on a dare, and are never consumed. Sometimes they get scorched. Often they get smudged with soot and ash so that they come to look shabby, like vagrants. High above them, buzzards turn in slow circles, lowering themselves in passes to the carcasses of the rabbits and rats run down by the flames. Sometimes, following the burning of an entire block, people from town come out to the fields and club rabbits in the weeds along the ditch banks.

4

The interests of the Florida sugar cane industry are seen to by the Florida Sugar Cane League, a trade association devoted to lobbying, research, and public relations. I had hopes of interviewing a number of cutters and touring the camps. I called the League from New York City and said that I planned to come down for a few weeks and look around, and the pleasant young woman in charge of public relations said there wouldn't be much point in that. "No one ever stays more than three days," she said. "They see a movie and visit a farm and get a tour of a mill and that's it." I said that I was particularly interested in meeting the West Indians and seeing the camps where they lived and how they spent their time after work and if it really was as hard to cut sugar cane as I'd heard and all the warmth drained from her voice and she said, "You will never meet a cutter or visit a camp." She said that the cutters didn't like being disturbed. She asked if I had a camera and I said that I did and she said that the cutters hated being photographed. Furthermore, she said the growers had had it with articles highlighting conditions at the camps and the rigors of the fields and the hardships endured by the cutters. In beginning to look into the sugar business I had collected a booklet published during the nineteen-forties by U.S. Sugar under the title *The Everglades: Agro-Industrial Empire of the South*, which contained this sentence: "On both sides of the highway west from Belle Glade can be seen the South Bay Plantation of the United States Sugar Corporation, with its neat, orderly, and well-maintained cottages of the happy, contented plantation workers." So I felt as if the attitude I was dealing with had a historical reference.

When I first went to Florida I always checked in with the League, because the people there were pleasant and helpful and then I began to realize it was not in my interest to do so. Whenever I called a person in the industry he would ask if I had got clearance from the League to make the call, or say he couldn't talk without checking with the League, or say the information I wanted would have to come from the League. Then he would call the League and tell them I had contacted him. A woman I know called a friend who worked for one of the growers and asked if he could arrange for me to watch cutters in the fields. The League heard about it and called her up and said she had no authority to arrange an introduction for me. The person I was to have been introduced to then called my friend and said he would not meet me unless it had been cleared with the League.

I had an introduction to a Haitian man in Belle Glade who

worked for the Florida Rural Legal Services and said he could spare half an hour one afternoon to take me to meet some cutters. His name was Jackson François. He said we could probably talk to a few Jamaicans, but mostly we would have to talk to Haitians, because that was who he knew; each year a few dozen Haitians from the area find work in the harvest. We drove to the camp in the center of Belle Glade. Cutters stared at us from the balcony and stood around on the street. Laundry hung from the railings. We approached three cutters standing on the sidewalk. Jackson's greeting was jaunty. The cutters said nothing. Jackson pointed to one and turned to me saying, "You can talk to him." I asked the man if he cut sugar cane and he just looked at me. The cutters began taunting Jackson for appearing well-to-do. Jackson said, "You have a good job, you make more than me, we all do different jobs, sometimes I can do your job and you can do mine, but you make more than me." One of them turned to me and said he wanted money to talk about sugar cane. He asked where I was from, and when I said New York City he said that I should have brought women. He said if I wanted to talk to anyone about sugar cane I must bring money and women. Furthermore, he said, if I wanted to talk to a Jamaican, I must bring a Jamaican, not a Haitian.

We walked over to some cutters leaning against a car. Jackson pointed to one and said, "You want to talk to this man?" I said yes and Jackson said, "You can talk to him." I asked the man if he cut cane and he said yes and looked away. I asked how he had started and he said, "I don't know myself." The man who had insisted on money came over and said, "Pay me money to talk about cutting cane." When I didn't say anything, he turned to Jackson and said, "Pay me money to tell him about cane." Jackson saw a Haitian he knew standing by himself and went over to him. The man was perhaps ten feet from the others. He had just come from the fields. He was wearing a red bandanna on his head. He said that he had cut cane for three seasons. "You cut cane and you put it on the floor," he said. "A field walker tells you where to cut and he tells you how much price you will be paid for the task. If you don't know how to cut the first time, they teach you how to do it." Then, "I am going to quit. After I finish the season. It is no good job. They don't take care of you if you get sick. If you die, they don't care. The work is hard, and the pay not enough. If you feel good for the day and you work hard, you can make some money. That the devil way of the sugar cane."

We went back to the group of Jamaicans. I thought that perhaps since they had now seen one man talk to us they might give up asking for money and talk themselves. They said we must have permission from their supervisor. Jackson said, "No, we want to talk to you." He took a pad of paper out of his pocket and flipped the pages, appearing to look for something, as a prop. The cutters just stood there watching him. We found the supervisor in the back of the camp, talking to a woman. He said we could not talk to the cutters without the permission of the company and that if we were going to talk to a cutter about the work we should talk to him in the fields. Jackson said it was not possible to call a man from his work and the supervisor said, "What I said, and I'm not going to withdraw on this, is the best place for you is the field." Then he put his hands in his pockets and walked away from us. Jackson said, "They wish the brain not to say anything."

We walked back to the street. Jackson said he had a friend named Horace, a Jamaican who lived in the camp, and we could talk to him, but it would have to be some other day, since he was now out of time.

5

The soil on which most of the sugar cane is grown is flammable. Once ignited, it is not easily extinguished. Soil fires have a tendency to smolder. A man in Clewiston owns land that caught fire soon after he bought it and burned for three years. The soil is called muck and is composed of leaves and branches and vines and trees only partially decayed. Mainly it is swamp bottom from which the water has been drained. (Soil less decomposed than muck is peat.) It gives underfoot like a cushion. Standing in a muck field near a place where a cutter drops a bundle of cane you feel the shock. After a rain, the soil is a rich black, like a pigment; it almost shines. People call it black gold. Dry, it is gray and powdery. Growers liken it to talcum or feathers and say that you sink to your shoe tops in it. Tractors disking the fields in preparation for planting stir up clouds of it that rise and hang in sheets on the wind.

People noticed in clearing the land that the soil gave them a rash and that sometimes the rash developed sores. The rash they called muck sting. Against it, supervisors wore high boots, riding britches, and khaki shirts buttoned at the wrist, and field hands wore gloves and tied the cuffs of their trousers with string. Whatever accounted for the rash has been depleted by cultivation, but muck still contains a lot of bacteria; a man who receives a cut while working on the muck is immediately treated for infection.

Because the land is so flat the fields lose practically no soil to erosion. What soil they lose is to a process called subsidence: microorganisms turn the organic matter in the soil into carbon dioxide and water. Subsidence proceeds at a rate of about one inch a year. Beneath the muck is limestone. How much muck remains in a field can be determined by driving along a canal and noting the depth of the soil above the rock.

There are three kinds of muck—custard apple, also called Okeechobee muck, sawgrass, also called Everglades peat, and willow-and-elder, also called Okeelanta peaty muck. Each derives its principal name from the trees that grew above it; custard apples and sawgrass grew widely in particular areas, and willows and elders grew in pockets among them. Places where the lake overflowed the land are richest in minerals and nutrients, particularly nitrogen, and soil there is less vulnerable to subsidence. Custard apple trees grew closest to the lake. Custard apple muck is the most productive but accounts for the smallest acreage under cultivation; most of it lies beneath the stores and houses of Belle Glade. The bulk of the muck under cultivation is sawgrass.

Most of the muck lies to the south and east of the lake.

As one travels farther from it the minerals diminish. West of Clewiston the only patch of muck is a strip about a mile wide running west from close to the lake to near the old mill at Moore Haven. All around it is sand.

Perhaps sixty per cent of the soil under cultivation is muck. The rest is either sand, or some mixture of sand and muck. Muck that has undergone subsidence to the extent that it now includes sand is called sandy muck, or salt-and-pepper muck, or black sand. Sandy soil composed of the smallest grains is called ball-bearing sand and is untillable; the grains will not support upright the weight of the cane. The sand by itself is not fertile; chemicals make it so. Some of the sand land once supported cattle. When that failed to pay, growers began putting sugar cane on it.

Muck produces an abundance of cane, but not necessarily cane with a high amount of sugar. Nitrogen stimulates growth but inhibits the production of sucrose. On new muck land, particularly land that has first been used as pasture, a grower will likely get vigorous growth and low sugar. Until the elements of the soil can be brought into balance with fertilizers, the sugar recovered will be low in relation to the production of the field.

Growing sugar cane on muck is less expensive than growing it on sand because muck needs less fertilizer. Also, muck holds water. Sand drains quickly, so requires more water, therefore the fields have more ditches. Because less of the field is lost to ditches, growers can plant more sugar cane per acre on muck. On sand there are ditches perhaps as often as every fourteen rows. On muck there may be a ditch every hundred and twenty rows, perhaps every two hundred. Each ditch takes the space of four rows.

Muck fields are most often square, and sand fields long and narrow. Sand rows are usually half a mile long, whereas muck rows tend to be a quarter. Muck rows are shorter in order to lessen the distance the loaded wagons travel across the softer soil; a stuck wagon can tear a sizeable hole in a field.

Fields are divided by roads and headlands and canals into blocks. A headland is the strip of land between the end of the field and the road. On sand, because of the ditches, the blocks are smaller. On muck there tend to be fifty to sixty-four acres to a block. On sand there can be as few as six or seven. If a grower decides that he needs another canal in a block he will lay it through the middle of the field, and this is called splitting the field. Longer rows on sand mean more work for the burners.

Although sand produces fewer tons of cane, the cane it grows tends to produce more sugar. In addition, a grower on sand land can interrupt the supply of nitrogen, which will shock the cane into generating more sugar. A grower on muck land can't do this. On sand, four returns of a field is good. On muck, a planting can return as often as twelve seasons; at least one has reached twenty-two. What declines is not the amount of sugar in a stalk, but the tonnage of the field.

Some growers believe that any defects in a field can be overcome by fertilizers. Others contribute as little as possible to the field, feeling that every amount spent on fertilizer is money from their pockets. Some growers believe they can keep the returns high over the years on a field by controlling the amount and the schedule of the applications of fertilizer. They try to strike some balance between returns on the field and the cost of fertilizers.

At the moment when a field has reached the point where it can no longer be farmed—that is, when the depth of soil over limestone is too shallow to permit cultivation—it is turned into pasture. Men and women sitting at desks at the Florida Sugar Cane League and in offices at the corporations and behind the wheels of tractors and pickup trucks and jeeps in the fields occasionally wonder what the hell will be done with all that land when the muck disappears.

6

If you go out to the fields and lie down for a while, you draw the attention of buzzards. Sometimes one passes so close that you can look him in the eye and see that he is looking at you, and you can see the way the feathers at the end of his wingtips move like fingers, and you can hear the rushing, streamlined noise he makes in parting the air. Late in the afternoon buzzards swarm in huge, intricate formations high in the air, like a stunt. In one formation I counted two hundred and twenty-six; they were so far away their bodies looked like tiny black crosses. The looping, swirling, back-and-forth patterns they traced in their flight looked like the model of something from chemistry. A buzzard moving through the air makes a lot of noise, and as I watched them I tried to imagine the sound hundreds of them were making up there where nobody could hear it. A person can find a field being cut the same way a fisherman locates fish in open water, by watching the sky for birds. Egrets chase the fires and the mechanical harvesters. Buzzards follow the rice trucks bringing the cutters their lunch then lower themselves to the plates the cutters have discarded. Jamaicans call the buzzards John Crows. While they work, the buzzards wheel above them. Occasionally their shadows cross the road in front of your car. They are clumsy on the ground. In taking off they struggle to lift themselves into the air. They look as if flying were difficult and they had not practiced lately.

Wild turkeys live among the cane rows. Jeckyl birds scratch the fields for grubs and pick up rice from the plates before the buzzards arrive. Redwing blackbirds sail into the fields, their tails spread like fans, as if they were posing for a postcard. Owls hunt rats on the headlands. Hawks scan the crop rows from the power lines or perch like hood ornaments on top of the railroad cars that carry cane to the mill; in gaining the air they first fall forward, then climb in a long rising curve, tracing a line like a checkmark. After a sudden rain swallows hunt insects drawn to the heated pavement of the highway. They make a shrill, strident cry like a ringing in the ears or taut wires being struck. You sometimes see their carcasses lodged in the grillwork of cars parked in town. In between fires egrets gather in flocks so large and stationary that they look like a crop. They are called flatheads, or cattle egrets or cow birds, because they follow the cattle. In the evening they settle in numbers onto the fields like water birds onto a lake.

7

For the most part, the cutting of sugar cane is performed in the absence of white men. The cut foreman is in charge. Under his eye work the leadmen and the ticket writers, all past cutters who excelled.

The row price comes from the grower to the cutters by way of the cut foreman, also called the crew leader. He carries out the grower's instructions on what fields to harvest, and in the case of fields damaged by frost, passes on the information of where on the stalk the cut should be made. If he sees a man cutting recklessly, he will remind him of sound practices. Some cutters feel encumbered by the equipment; when they get a ways down the field they take it off; if the cut foreman finds them he will have them put it back on. The leadmen, also called field walkers, also called pushers, announce the row price to the cutters. (Ticket writers also do this.) If a cutter is leaving his stubble too high, or has too many tops in his pile, or is piling in a disorganized way, the pusher will call him back to correct his work. The pusher walks up and down the rows chopping back stubble and keeping the rows piled neatly. The ticket writers record the hours a cutter has worked and how much he has cut. If a cutter is working too slowly, the ticket writer has the authority to remove him from the field, what is called checking him out. A cutter loses any wages he has earned on a day he is checked out. In the past a man called a scrapper followed the continuous loader, the machine that picks up the cane, gathering stalks it had missed and transferring them to rows waiting to be collected. The scrapper was selected from among the slowest cutters. A few years ago it was decided that the scrapper, who was paid by the hour, did not earn his wage in cane retrieved.

Crews amount usually to no fewer than twenty-five cutters and not more than fifty; it is difficult for a ticket writer to keep track of more. There are no two-way radios in the fields; when a ticket writer (or a leadman, or a cutter) has something to tell another down the rows, he shouts. Sometimes, when the two are far apart, the message is picked up by voices in between and passed on.

If they have been cutting sloppily in favor of speed, cutters do not complain at being sent back to clean up their work. Otherwise they resent it. It is not possible for the sugar left behind in the stalk to be recovered; the loader picks up only lengths of cane, not chips. Furthermore, it is someone else's job to make sure the field is left attractive to the grower's eye, should he ride by after the harvest. Cutters say that calling them back is a practice leadmen abuse; they say that leadmen employ it to slow down a cutter who might be making more money that day than the leadman.

Cane rows are five feet apart. Two men line up at four rows. Each lays the stalks he cuts across the inside two rows and throws his trash on the outside row. The rows in which he piles his cane are called pile rows or heaprows or windrows. The outside row is his trash pile. On a finished field the pile rows alternate with the rows of trash like stripes on a flag. Cutters work often in pairs. A faster man handicaps a man cutting slower because the stalks the faster man piles often spill into the slower man's row and must be cleared aside before the man working slower can make his cut. Likewise, having to cut and pile carefully in order to keep clear of the slower man's row costs the faster man time. Furthermore, a slower man can impede a faster if the cane he is cutting falls into the faster man's row. Two men working together are pile partners; in addition each has a trash partner, but this relation is coincidental and has no effect on his speed, because even should they fall into his row, tops and leaves are no obstacle to the blade. Often a faster man will walk ahead to free himself of a cutter whose stalks are falling in his row.

Some pairs form spontaneously, some by the accident of where a cutter lines up, and some are long-standing. Over the course of a season few remain intact; the rate at which a man cuts is not stable over time and is not likely to keep pace with another's. The etiquette of the fields is that a cutter must give up his row if another arrives during line-up and says he is the partner of the man in the neighboring row. An ideal pair would include a left-handed and a right-handed cutter. Each will line up with his cutting hand outside, so he doesn't have to pull the cane across his body to pile it.

Cutters remove the leaves and the tops. Leaves contain mainly water and little sugar and the tops have no sugar. In addition, the tops contain a wax that interferes with milling. Damage from frost begins at the top of the stalk and descends; in a frost-damaged field the grower shows the foreman, who shows the leadmen, what portion of the stalk to discard.

The only things left undisturbed in the fields are fire ant mounds and stalks of dog fennel and Napier grass; the cutters touch nothing that doesn't make them money. Napier grass they call bamboo, because that is what it looks like (it also looks like sugar cane). The white people call it maiden cane, because it is left by itself in the field.

Cutters are morbidly fearful of snakes. They believe that only a fool or a man who cared little for his life would accept the existence of such a thing as a snake that is not fatally poisonous. A cutter who sees a snake sunning itself on the bank of a canal will often interrupt what he is doing to find a rock to drop on it. The bravest among them will kill any snake they see in the fields on behalf of the crew by beating it with a cane stalk. They believe that if they were to use their knives they would poison themselves later in bringing a residue of venom on the blade into contact with a stalk they were cutting to chew.

The ability of sugar cane to return from previous plantings is called ratooning. Some people in Florida call it retooning, and it is not possible to tell if they mean it ironically. Ratooning is also called stubbling back. A crop obtained from a field planted the previous season is called a plant crop. The next crop is called the first stubble crop and so on. The older a field, the more difficult it is to cut. Cutters make their cut at the base of the stalk, as close to the ground as possible. If the stubble was left too high the year before, there may be some remnant of it for the cutter's blade to pass through before reaching the stalk. Moreover, the stalks return thinner, the cane falls over. This is called sprawling. Cane also sprawls from rats having gnawed the stalks, and because fire weakens the fiber in the stems, and because cane taller than about eight feet falls over anyway. The growing season being so long in south Florida, just about the entire crop sprawls. Cane that has sprawled continues to grow, sometimes to a length of seventeen feet, and in the process to weave itself among other stalks in the row. Sometimes it takes another root. Wind tangles sprawled cane. Cane that has sprawled in all directions and tangled itself up is called rooster tail cane. A grower must pay slightly more to have cane of this type cut or risk trouble from his crews. With rooster tail cane there are sometimes three cuts to the stalk, instead of two, in order to make the curved stalks lie flat in their pile rows. In rooster tail cane the fastest man is no faster than the slowest. Cane that grows straight, which is to say plant cane, is called soldier cane.

The decision of which end to start cutting a field at is made by noting which way the cane lies. The cut proceeds in the direction it points, so the cutter has not got to stand up the stalks in order to make his cut. Sometimes cane falls in the direction of the pile; cutters call this a fall-in row. Cane that falls away from the pile and has to be carried forms a dragover row. In a row where stretches of cane lie against the grain of the field a cutter will sometimes cut those places first, then collect the rest of the row. Walking up the row to cut cane that falls away from the pile row is called backing the cane.

The cutters ride to and from the fields in schoolbuses. The larger growers often have land in more than one county; it is not unusual for cutters to travel twenty-five miles to a field. Once the buses arrive in the fields the cutters from their seats begin scanning the rows. What they are looking for are rows that thin out or have gaps. Once the bus stops they race to them. A lot of accidents involving the knife take place during the rush to leave the bus and claim a row. Sometimes a row that looks lean from the front bears more heavily farther into the field, and a row that begins heavy can hit a place where lightning struck or the ground is not level and standing water has killed off the cane. Rarely a cutter gets lucky and finds a row that is lean to the end. Rarely, because growers do not raise sugar cane to bear lightly.

Time for which a cutter must be paid begins when he steps off the bus. If no work is available, which might happen toward the end of the day, the grower will often have him carried to the camp, otherwise he must pay him for the time he spends in the fields. When the growers move cutters from a field on one side of the camp to one on another, they have them taken by a route that does not carry them past the barracks in order not to tempt them with quitting for the day. Cutters slow down after lunch. A grower who wants a lot of work done fast will schedule it for the morning, then hold up the rice truck.

From the grower the cutters each receive a water jug which they fill and bring to the fields. At smaller camps the cooks freeze ice for them. Sometimes the cutters fill the jugs with juice they make from water and syrups they buy in the supermarkets. Strawberry cordial is a favorite syrup. The cutters leave the jugs at the head of the row, then return for them when they get farther down the field. The grower leaves a water wagon in the field for refills. When the cutters finish their rows they head off in search of another or for the bus, walking with the jugs balanced on their heads. With their eyes staring into the distance they look as if the landscape they see in their minds is not the one through which they are walking.

The strongest cutters pace themselves and work with equal vigor all day. Once they finish a row they line up at another. If the rows are light they can line up as many as four times.

Cutters have a distaste for the grime of the fields. The cane when it burns forms a gum on its stalk of carbonized sugar, which is sticky and when mixed with the ash turns black, like pitch. The cutters come away from the stalks smeared with this mixture, so that after a few hours their clothing is black on one side of their bodies from shoulder to knee. They often close the top buttons of their collars and tie their shirt cuffs at the wrist so the cane top doesn't chafe them and also so the paste doesn't stain their skin. Some wear two pairs of pants, or an outer pair cut off at the knee. "If I do not dress in two pants," a cutter told me, "I be blacker than I black already." Many wear hats to keep the dirt from their hair and also because the cane fibers irritate their scalps. Some wear bandannas tied across their faces against the ash and dust. They believe that breathing the ash from the fields is unwholesome. They think that it fills up their lungs and shortens their lives. Many grow beards to protect their faces against the dirt and the cold, and because they believe a beard gives them strength.

At the end of the day, covered with the ash and the sap and the dirt of the fields, they smell of sweat and sugar.

A cutter is expected to cut eight tons a day, which the majority can do in six hours. The most capable can manage ten and a half. How many tons of cane there are to a row varies among fields, but as an approximate rule there is a ton of cane to every three hundred feet of cut row.

On days when the demands of the mill are extraordinary, cutters sometimes work into the evening. When the light in the fields is not sufficient to let them see what they are doing, they work by the headlights of the buses.

At the start of the harvest the cutters are issued a pair of canvas gloves with leather palms. The gloves last perhaps a week, maybe ten days, and are expensive to replace. Most work without them. Under the abrasion of the handle of the knife the cutters' palms blister, then callus deeply. Over the course of the season they stiffen and become smooth; they feel like linoleum. The cutters apply lotion to them to keep the surface from cracking. Once they are home the hand takes weeks to return to usefulness. It causes them pain up their arms to the shoulder and it cramps. They rub Ben-Gay on it for pain and wintergreen oil to relax it and see a doctor if it refuses to heal.

8

The Florida Sugar Cane League shows a film they had made for the purposes of lobbying and public relations which includes a scene of a sugar cane cutter at work, while a narrator says, "To watch a West Indian wield a cane knife is to see a centuries-old art." A person might come away from this film pleased with knowing an abstruse, *National Geographic*–type fact about the islands in the West Indies: men there happen to excel without effort at the rather obscure and dangerous task of cutting sugar cane, the way people somewhere else excel at holding their breath for long periods of time, which makes them exceptional pearl divers.

Because this film is made for the purposes of lobbying and public relations and is describing harvest practices involved in an area of America where the harvest has traditionally been carried out by black people, it contains an additional implication: Isn't it remarkable that black men in America simply lack this skill, just plain flat don't have it, but, no wonder, it's an *exotic* skill, and we have to go to an exotic (and backward) place to obtain artisans still capable of performing it. The film does not say anything about the circumstances of the life of the man whose image appears on the screen, which one might guess include distress to the extent that he is willing to endure the hardships and dangers of the cane fields, the loneliness of living away from home for almost half of the year while his children grow up without him, while his family changes and forms alliances that it will take him some time to penetrate, if he is able to at all, and the worry over whether the woman with whom he shares some intimacy might possibly be sharing herself with another man. It says nothing about sorrow. Nor does it acknowledge the offensiveness of its observation. Another way of framing the sentiment of the narrator's remark is to say, "To watch an American Negro pick cotton is to watch a centuries-old art." Furthermore, it is simply wrong. Very few West Indian men have ever held a cane knife before arriving in Florida.

At the start of the season cutters are given eight days to learn to cut cane. The growers are allowed to request sixty per cent of their cutters from the previous year. The reason for the stipulation being that the positions are coveted in the West Indies, where jobs are so scarce and wages so low; this arrangement is a compromise among West Indian politicians who control the right to hand out invitations to interviews as patronage, their governments, which would like to spread the opportunity as widely as possible, and the growers, whose interest is in assembling the most capable work force. Among the forty per cent who do not receive invitations to return are some who reapply and are accepted, which means that each year somewhere between twenty-five and forty per cent of the cutters are cutting cane for the first time. During the eight-day period cutters are paid an hourly wage. Or they can choose to work at the piece rate. Experienced cutters often accept the hourly rate and use this time to work themselves into shape. If they hit their pace early they can slack off, since no matter what their production their pay is the same. During the period of training the growers note the cutters who are struggling, which does not require any close attention; the field after an hour or so looks like a track on which a race is in progress. Once the eight days are up, the contract permits the growers to test a cutter's production. Some growers measure a length of cane and require the cutter to harvest it in a certain amount of time. Some measure his production over the course of an hour. If a cutter fails to meet a standard, the grower can remove him from the field, can check him out. A cutter can be checked out for a variety of reasons—the pusher may decide the cutter is piling sloppily, or leaving too many tops, or too much stubble in the field—but if he is checked out three times for lack of production, he can be sent home. If this should happen before half of the season has expired, the cutter must pay the cost of his ticket over and back. If he manages to remain past the halfway point, the grower pays his transportation. To be certain of remaining on the contract a cutter must regularly harvest a minimum of one ton an hour.

The period of instruction is brief. Painstaking growers might show the cutters a field cut to standard by their lead men, the rows piled carefully as cordwood, the stubble cut low and clean. More likely the lead men will only demonstrate the elements of cutting: stepping forward with the foot on the side of one's cutting hand (keeping the other foot back and clear of the blade on its follow-through); bending over and wrapping an arm around a bunch of stalks and raising the blade up over the shoulder and bringing it down hard across one's body to the field, striking the cane at the base of the stalk; shaving the tops from the stalks with short, flicking strokes; piling; and knowing the moment to brace the end of the knife against the toe of one's boot and run the file past it to sharpen it. He might tell them not to cross the pile rows (which are slippery) while holding a knife, and that if they have to jump a ditch they should throw their knives over first. Then he might cut a few feet of cane, saying, "You got to learn to cut your stubble low, pile the cane straight, cut the top them off, and make a trash pile."

Once a cutter has learned to cut stubble low and pile the cane and keep neat separate rows and to swing the blade with the least resistance and to know the moment to stop work and sharpen his blade, the task becomes a matter of concentration. He must put his mind on speed and a rhythm that consumes the least of his energy. Letting his mind drift to the question of whether the man who sells him bottled gas for his stove is knocking at his door with a gift may mean experiencing the sudden sight of his blood.

9

I obtained an introduction to an ex-con named Caveman, who drove a tractor for one of the growers. He had a small, strutty, high-strung friend named Anthony, who also drove a tractor, and sometimes accompanied us when we went out looking for cutters.

They picked me up one afternoon at the Inn, driving Anthony's car, which had a door on one side that was a different color from the rest of the car. Caveman said, "Let my chauffeur drive, I'll sit in the back." We had traveled two blocks when Anthony remembered that the retread on his right front tire was about to let go, so we drove back to the hotel and picked up my rental car, which was some kind of American car with a dashboard that looked like the instrument panel in an airplane. Anthony settled himself behind the wheel and said, "This car *fits* me. I like this car."

We drove west, in the direction of Moore Haven, slipping past the McDonald's and the Burger King and the K-Mart and the high school and the houses and the motels and the hospital and the police car parked in the median with a mannequin at the wheel to scare speeders and the airport and the golf course and the Sugar Cane League and over the railroad tracks leading from the fields to the mill and into the vast panorama of cane towards Shawnee Farm, which the cutters call Shiny Farm and the local black people call Chinee Farm, or Chinese Farm.

"You don't have no kind of benefit cutting cane, cause it's *piece* work," Anthony said. "It going to be *rough* now too, since it turning cold."

"That frost *hurt* the cane," Caveman said. "They get frost and it be white in the morning, then the sun come out and heat it up. It get *sweet*." Then he said, "You make a good chauffeur, Anthony."

"I got a sister damn near a genius," Anthony said.

Shawnee is a village of Homosote cabins built on stilts in the shade of some oaks about eight miles west of Clewiston and a mile from the Lake. The cabins are arranged along a road in the shape of a horseshoe. Anthony drove slowly past them. On the porch of one a cutter without a shirt stood at the sink, washing his cane knife. Anthony stopped the car and Caveman called him over. He walked toward us carrying his knife dripping water from the blade. Caveman asked if he cut cane.

He said, "Yeah, I cut some cane."

A man was watching us from the window of the house. He called something to the man we were talking to. The man turned from his waist and I noticed that he had a muscle in his back where I had never seen one before.

Caveman said, "You work seven days?"

"Yes."

Caveman looked at me. There was a silence. Then Caveman nodded to the cutter and Anthony drove ahead. Caveman said, "I was going to talk to the man, but I don't know what it is you want to know, so I didn't know what to ask."

Anthony took us back to the county road. "I did that cane cutting one time," he said. "About thirty minutes. I was going through that cane, chopping it, chop, chop, chop, and I said, 'Hey, man, this ain't no job for you.'"

I asked what he did the rest of the year. He said, "In the off season I haul ass to Alabama and play all the girls I can play. I a *sea*sonal man."

Anthony thought it might be a good idea for us to go down to Belle Glade and look for cutters there. I said that Belle Glade had looked to me like a rough town. Anthony said, "It ain't all *looks*. It's for real. That's the Jamaican capital." He pronounced Jamaican the way a lot of black people in south Florida do, "Jew-maican." Then he said, "The Jamaican thinks he's smart. You can't tell him nothing. They smart. They *too* smart."

First we drove to the Benbow Camp, out by the levee. Anthony brought us around the back out of sight of the supervisor's office by the entrance. We parked and walked over to a group of cutters standing beside their house. A numbers runner among them was writing down bets on a pad, like a waiter. The runners have territories. A small camp might belong to one runner; at a larger camp one might have only a building, or a floor, or the men of a particular island. The payoff is based on the running of the dogs at a track in Miami. When the runner was done, Caveman asked the others if they would mind if I asked some questions. One of the cutters said, "Ask," but when he saw that I was going to write down what he said, he told us that we had to go first and see the bossman.

We got back in the car and drove farther into the camp. Caveman said he knew someone who lived in it. We parked again. Caveman saw two men leaning against a car outside a bunkhouse. He said, "Hey, where Robbie Lee stay?"

"Down there with the blue car in the yard."

"He home?"

"I don't know."

We got in the car and Anthony drove us in the direction the man had pointed. Anthony said, "Which blue car? That one there?"

Caveman said, "Yeah, that the Robbie Lee car right there."

We got out and talked to a man standing by the car. He was an American, perhaps a bus driver. Caveman said, "You know a little about that cane, don't you?" and the man said, "Hell, no, I don't study that at all."

A man carrying a toolbox came around the corner of the house. Anthony said, "You pull cane?" and the man said, "I don't know a damn thing about it."

Caveman took me aside and said, "They *know* it, but they won't talk it."

Anthony said, "You all got the girls occupied out here?"

The man with the toolbox said, "We ain't got no girls out here."

Anthony turned away and said, "Yeah, tell that stuff to somebody else."

We were standing by the houses for the field walkers. A woman banged open the screen door of one and started across the road. Anthony brightened. He said, "Hey, Miss, you going to be occupied this weekend?"

She said, "I'm occupied all the time."

Anthony said, "Damn, I think I should have put on my Michael Jackson suit."

From inside the house a woman's voice said, "Hey, Caveman."

Anthony said, "Somebody know you, Cave."

The woman said, "Caveman, get over here."

Caveman said, "Yes, ma'am."

He went into the house and came out a moment later, saying he had asked them if they wanted to say anything about sugar cane and they said, "Yeah, it's hell out there."

Anthony walked back to the car to get his sunglasses. A young woman came out the door of one house, then crossed a small yard to another. Anthony said, "Man, this camp got so many pretty women." Then, "Yo, baby, get that frown off your face!"

We went to the supervisor's house. His name, we had been told, was Justin Brown, and Caveman knocked on the door and asked the boy who answered it, "Is Brown home?" We stepped inside the kitchen, which was dark. There was a clock on the far wall and a plaster crucifix and a set of praying hands on a table. Brown said that we would have to talk to the head office before I could speak to any of the cutters. He was friendly, though. He asked Anthony's name and then Caveman's, then said, "Caveman . . . *Cave*man," and started laughing.

On our way out the door Anthony called Caveman by his given name, saying, "That man *knows* you from someplace, Willie."

We got back in the car. Anthony said, "I'll bring you through some cane, man." Then he asked how I knew about sugar cane and I told him I had heard about it in New York. "All the way up there," he said. "Somebody went all the way up to New York City from Florida, Cave. Might be some brother."

Caveman nodded. He said he knew a Barbadian who had arrived on the contract, then married an American woman. He thought the man might talk to me. Anthony said, "Those Barbadians, they'll get over here to cut cane, but they don't like it that much. They'll cut cane to *get* here, but they don't care too much about that cane. The thing is to *stay* here."

We drove a while. The fields shimmered in the heat. An alligator sunned itself on a drainpipe emptying into a canal. Anthony said, "Cave, you remember that man marry Sandy, or going with Sandy, he used to work for the cement company—no—he work for the city?"

"You talking about Sam?"

"No."

"Short guy?"

"No, he ain't that short."

"I called him Jew-Boy? You ever heard me call a Jamaican Jew-Boy? That was him."

"Yeah, that him. All the Jamaican want to marry American women."

"I think I could marry six or seven sometime."

"Damn, that be bigamy. Ain't that what they call it, Cave?"

"Yeah."

"You need to be over in Africa to do that, living to be a hundred, with one hundred babies and one hundred wives."

10

Beside the Sugarland Highway, across from the Golf View Motel, a little toward Moore Haven, was a field that one year was half as tall as the others around it. What had happened is a man and a woman from Jamaica had robbed the Stop and Go in Clewiston and escaped by car. A couple of hours later the woman returned to the store and bought some things and was recognized. She gave the name of the man to the police, who rounded him up. During the trip to the jail in Labelle, he complained that his handcuffs were too tight. The deputy loosened them. The Jamaican got one hand free and grabbed the deputy's gun and got out of the car by the railroad tracks and disappeared into the cane. A number of other cops arrived, summoned by the deputy. They brought dogs with them and sent one into the field. The Jamaican shot him and after that the deputies weren't able to convince any of the other dogs to go into the field, so the deputies set fire to it. No one saw the Jamaican come out. He had, but under cover of the smoke, and had crossed into another field. As the deputies were about to give up the search, the Jamaican crossed the highway, firing shots. One of the deputies chased him and shot him in the leg as the Jamaican was climbing the far bank of a canal.

Sometime during the evening it had come to be thought that Caveman had driven the getaway car. He had no idea how the police had arrived at this conclusion, because he was already serving time in Labelle when they brought the Jamaican in.

11

Sugar cane is grown not from seed but from cuttings. A grower selects a field in which the stand is pure and uses the stalks to plant other fields. Seed cane is cut in the fall by West Indians who have married American women and become residents, as well as by Haitians, but mainly by cutters requested early on the contract. It is particularly arduous work, because of the heat, and because the cane is cut green, and it usually pays twice the rate of the harvest.

There are two kinds of planting: successive and winter. Fields planted successively are those that have lain fallow for a season and been planted in the fall. Winter-planted fields are ones planted just after harvest. Between harvest and planting they are disked to kill off as much as possible of the old planting, which might harbor disease. Successive fields usually produce more cane, because they have a longer season, although they may lose some of their growth to a freeze. Planting ends with the frost, when the seed cane dies.

Seed cane is drawn from successively planted fields. A grower taking cane from a winter-planted field could never be sure of the purity of his stand—that is, he could never be certain he had cleansed it of its earlier crop.

About half the growers are particular about the quality of seed cane they use; the rest use whatever is at hand.

The fields are planted mostly by Haitians but also by Mexicans. Planting is day labor. Haitian crews are assembled each morning before dawn in a run-down part of Belle Glade at a square called the ramp. A number of growers send buses to the ramp before daylight. Their drivers hire the planters and bring them to the fields. The process of hiring is chaotic. In addition to the sugar companies' buses there are buses at the ramp gathering crews for work in the vegetable harvest. Some men and women work regularly for one company or another and board its bus and sit down and wait. Many work in vegetables one day and sugar cane the next, or for one grower one day and another the next, depending on the price. Or work a few days and build up some money and ease off, then return to scrambling for work. So a lot of people are running back and forth in the darkness trying to locate the best price for the lightest task. The buses begin filling up; the people start running faster and shouting more. Some of the drivers know certain workers and refuse them, so maybe there are arguments. By the time the sun has come up the buses are gone; the people who didn't find work have disappeared; the ramp is just an empty lot surrounded by slummy buildings.

Some growers use Mexican crews. They contract with a crew leader for a certain number of planters or a specific acreage. If the grower doesn't think a particular man is doing right, he tells the crew leader, who runs the man off. The leader is paid by the acre and the planters are paid by the row. In addition the leader receives a price for transportation; usually he has a bus and picks up the planters where they live. The leader supplies them with drinking water. Some of the crew members are Mexican-Americans from Texas. On days after the Immigration and Naturalization Service has pulled a raid, the crews are frequently depleted.

A crew plants four rows at a time. The seed cane is carried on a platform hauled slowly down the rows by a tractor. Two men stand at the back of the bed and each drops cane into the furrow that passes beneath him, and two men stand at the front of the bed, one on either side, and drop cane into the furrows beside them. Each drops two stalks at a time. The platform is followed by four choppers with machetes, who cut the stalks into sections; a sugar cane stalk resembles bamboo; there is a bud at each joint and if the stalks are not separated, a shoot will grow only from the terminal bud, the grower will get a poor root system and a thin field. The choppers swing the machetes casually; the blades come alarmingly close to their feet. They make a ringing sound in finding a rock. A man follows each crew to make sure the work is done properly.

The crews plant two and a half to four tons of seed cane per acre, depending on the grower's instructions. One crew might plant thirty-five to forty acres a day. The crews are often stable because they make their money by speed.

Planting is the only work of the fields in which women take part. Most often they are choppers. Along with the men they wear layers of clothes because when work begins the air is cold. They shed jackets and sweaters and shirts all day. The women often wear bright colors. They wrap scarves around their heads. They contribute the only displays of color to the fields.

Before planting, a field is made perfectly flat to prevent water from collecting. Standing water drowns the cane, leaving gaps in the field, and cane on high ground does poorly for the difficulty of reaching the water. Whether a field is sufficiently flat is determined by lasers.

Cane rows are planted five feet apart because over the years it has been decided that five feet allows light to reach the lower parts of the stalk, but not in such amounts that it encourages suckers—shoots that volunteer near the bottom of the stalk, sapping the plant's energy.

In new fields delivering especially thin stands, what are called skippy fields, or gappy fields—that is, fields with spaces of, say, three feet or more between stalks—a grower might decide to skip plant. Skip planting involves cutting a furrow between the stalks and replanting. It is expensive and takes up time and cuts the profit from the field. It is done early in the fall, when seed cane is still available. The grower needs to plant a variety that will grow quickly, because the rest of the field has a head start. The mills dislike handling a skip-planted field because it mixes varieties on them.

Some growers plant as close to the ditches and headlands as possible, in order to control weeds and provide extra cane. Since they are taxed on the gross acreage of their land, they use as much of it as they can. "If it's a piece of ground," I heard a grower say, "we're going to plant sugar on it." They keep the headlands clear to show up rats and snakes to owls and hawks.

A field receives four applications of fertilizer—March, May, July, and August. Exactly what to apply is determined in a commercial laboratory from a sample of the soil. Half of the first load is broadcast before planting, the rest is laid in the rows. The second is put on from a truck, the third from a truck or a plane, and the fourth from a plane.

On the muck, per acre, growers use between four hundred and five hundred pounds of fertilizer a season and on sand between fifteen hundred and twenty-one hundred, depending on the balance they want to strike between tons in the field and profit. Some growers try to average thirty-five tons per acre over the cycle of a field. They start with a plant crop of fifty tons, a first stubble of forty-five, second stubble of thirty-seven, and third of twenty-five to thirty. Others try for an average of fifty tons per acre. They receive about fifty-five tons per acre for their plant crop and then try against the odds to maintain the field with fertilizers. Thirty tons an acre is an average yield for sand, forty-five for muck.

With warm days and nights, cane germinates in two weeks. In cold, perhaps three. Occasionally it takes as many as six. Once the stalk appears, the growers scratch the field with cultivators to discourage the grass, which competes for water and fertilizer. Cane canopies in the early weeks of May, shutting out the light to the grass.

The fields are watered by seepage irrigation, fed by canals from the lake. Growers try to regulate the water table in such a way that the roots will have to seek it and grow deep and sturdy. If the table is too high, the roots might rot or grow too shallow to support the weight of the stalk. The best source of water is rain, which contains nitrogen. Growers hope for enough rain to nurture the fields—about a quarter of an inch a day—but not so much that the fertilizer will be washed into the canals.

Eighty-five- to ninety-degree weather through the summer, with eighty-five- to ninety-per-cent humidity until the middle of October, followed by cool nights and warm days until harvest, is ideal. Cane stops growing at sixty-eight degrees.

In south Florida what causes ripening in the cane is a drop in the temperature, which begins in September, but not early enough to stop growth and produce sugar in the cane scheduled for harvest in October. There are three things a grower on sand land can do early in the season to hurry up the ripening of the cane. He can withhold nitrogen from it, which will shock the plant into producing more sugar; he can withdraw the water from it, which will stop growth and produce more sugar but reduce tonnage; or he can apply chemicals. A grower on muck cannot regulate nitrogen, because it is an element of the soil, and he cannot withdraw water, because that would cause him to lose soil to subsidence. Growers apply two chemicals—Polaris and Polado—from the middle of September to the middle of October. These interrupt growth and cause the plant to concentrate on producing sugar. They are called ripeners, or ripening agents. How well they work has in part to do with the variety of cane. They are sprayed on fourteen days before the harvest. Polado kills cane and is used only on fields that will be replanted. On sand land Polaris occasionally kills cane, although it shouldn't. Several years ago the mill at Clewiston insisted that one grower use Polaris on fields cut before the first of the year. The following year the cane did not return and the grower had to replant.

12

Sugar cane in south Florida is grown mainly on farms of immense acreage. There is no example of a person with, say, twenty or thirty acres in cane, or even two or three hundred. A small cane farm is five hundred acres. The profit is not large, so the farms have to be.

Men who drive tractors, or operate harvesters, or work in some way in the fields often talk wistfully of owning a small cane farm, which is not a simple ambition. "To start a farm" (this is a man who operates a harvesting crew), "you will want thirty thousand tons of production; at forty tons an acre, and with a quarter to a fifth of the farm lying fallow each year, that's a thousand acres, which is two million for land. (You could cut the acreage in half, but you'd need about the same amount of equipment, so you might as well have the extra land.) You could get pretty well equipped to farm it, with some secondhand equipment, for about two hundred and fifty thousand dollars. You'd need three tractors, two large disks, plows, chisels, a bulldozer, a dragline, shop equipment and shop, a second-hand dumptruck, tools, a pickup, spray rigs, and scratchers. The problem is there are no local contractors you can call up and say, 'I have fifty hours' work here, can you come out and do it?' All the equipment's too expensive for anyone to be in that kind of business waiting for calls.

"Let's assume you've got sand land and can harvest it with machines. You'll need another two hundred and fifty thousand for harvesting equipment. (If you're not using machines, you've got to build barracks to the government regulations and feed the cutters and staff the camp, or you've got to contract with the mill for their labor.) In addition to your harvester a quarter of a million gets you two more tractors and some wagons for hauling cane, one water wagon, one fuel wagon, and a parts truck with toolboxes and oil. Out of a thousand acres, you'd have eight hundred in production, so that's thirty-two thousand tons a year; profit at six dollars a ton, which is reasonable, is one hundred and ninety-two thousand to put in your pocket after harvest and growing costs. And you better not be into the bank then, because you can figure the interest on two and a half million, and what you made doesn't cover it."

Approximately one hundred and thirty-five farmers grow sugar cane in south Florida. The five largest growers are corporations or cooperatives. The sixth largest is Joe Marlin Hilliard. Hilliard's farm was begun as a cattle ranch early in the century by his grandfather, who ran it with his sons, Marlin and Joe A. They began by homesteading and bought their first land in 1932, then kept buying east, which is how they arrived in Clewiston. Joe Marlin made the cattle ranch a cane farm in 1961 by planting two hundred and seventy-three acres. He might have planted more, but until the Cuban Revolution the amount of cane that could be grown in America was controlled by government quota. Cuba held the main allocation. The Florida industry was modest. Afterward it was not. Joe A., Joe Marlin's father, is still active in the operation of his cattle interests and occasionally involves himself in the running of the cane farm. Marlin Hilliard died in 1981; he was backing his jeep onto the highway and was run down by a truck. He left a bill for inheritance tax of twelve million dollars.

The Hilliards' farm contains one hundred and fifteen sections of land. A section is one square mile, six hundred and forty acres. The farm is large enough that different parts of it receive different measures of rainfall over the course of a year. People in that country say about the Hilliards, "They own half the world down here." Joe Marlin gets around the whole place about once a month. He has twelve thousand acres in sugar cane, close to twenty square miles, most of it on sand, all of it harvested mechanically.

The size alone of Hilliard's farm would make him a figure of importance in south Florida, but it has also been his contribution to present a successful model of mechanical harvesting. Ten years ago U.S. Sugar planned to double the capacity of its mill at Clewiston. The company itself had the acreage for a portion of the increase. Other growers, Joe Marlin among them, were asked to supply the rest. While he was happy to plant additional fields, he did not want to build barracks for the extra cutters. Since his new fields were on sand, he decided to try harvesting them by machine and managed to convince a few other growers to go in with him on the equipment. They formed a cooperative called Sugarland Harvesting.

The harvest of a field by machine costs half as much as by hand. There are no labor camps to support and no cutters to feed. A machine enters a field as soon as the fire is out; often the cane is inside the mill the same day. Cane cut by hand takes at least two days to reach the mill—it is burned one day and cut the next; frequently it is delivered the third. Machines harvest in all but the heaviest rains. Cutters will continue work begun before rain, but won't enter a field in the rain. What trash the machines leave behind spreads itself over the field, forming an obstacle to weeds. There is no need of a continuous loader; the mechanical harvester delivers its cane into a wagon hauled by a tractor. Since they cut the cane into smaller sections—called billets or batons—more can fit in a railroad car or a truck bed. Machines cut a field in a quarter the time.

Two objections are made to mechanical harvesting: the mills say the machines send them too much trash, and the growers say the harvesters tear up the fields. Trash is roots and dirt and tops and leaves and dead animals, mostly rabbits. Owners of a mill receiving, say, ten per cent trash, believe themselves to be operating at a loss ten per cent of the time. Furthermore, they say that trash is a thief. They say it steals sugar by absorbing juice during milling and drawing it off with the bagasse—what is left of the stalks and the leaves and the tops after they have been run through the mill. Moreover, they say it clogs their machinery, and that the dirt abrades their rollers, although this is more a problem with sand than with muck, which is too soft to be of much concern. Hand-cut cane is perhaps two per cent trash. Machine-cut is seven to ten.

A grower using mechanical harvesters has to plant more often to offset the decline of his fields. If he is converting to the use of machines, he needs to build new roads; farm trails through the fields are not sufficient for the constant passage of heavy equipment. He needs also to build a gravel pit for the maintenance of the roads and he needs a water truck to spray the roads to keep down the dust. He needs to build and staff a shop to service his new equipment. He needs the best drainage in his fields so that the harvesters don't bog. Machines waste land; the growers cannot plant too close to headlands or beside canals because the harvesters fall into them. Growers call this tax land, since they pay the government on it but get nothing from it. If there is cane on it, left from a field that has not yet been replanted since being harvested by hand, the grower sends a cutter down it, which is expensive.

The complaint is made by some of the mills that machines leave cane in the field. The mills say that machines do not cut the cane as close to the ground as the cutters do. There is a saying in the sugar business that your profit is in your stubble; the mills say that every half inch of stubble left in an acre equals half a ton of cane. They also say that mechanical harvesters smear fallen cane—that is, make a tearing cut that spews chips from the stalk and splatters juice into the field. They say that as many as three tons can be lost in a field by smearing.

Sugar cane is vulnerable to a specific bacterium, found in

the soil, which enters through a crack in the stalk made during a freeze, or during the fire, or by the wheels of the tractor or the continuous loader, or by way of the cut made for harvest. The bacteria feed on the sucrose, turning it into a jellylike substance called dextran. Because it is red, dextran is commonly called red rot. Less sugar is recovered from sugar cane contaminated by dextran. It also causes problems with purity. In the plant, it saps the vigor of the shoots.

Dextran forms fastest in heat and humidity. It can infect cane in one day. Intact cane resists invasion for up to three days. The longer the cane lies in the field or in the railroad cars or truck beds waiting for delivery to the mill, the more dextran develops.

Mills claim that cuts made by hand are clean and seal themselves, while cuts made by machine tear the stalks and leave opportunities for the bacteria. Machines cut cane into billets half as long as ones cut by hand. This, the mills say, offers two more places for the bacteria to enter. This may or may not be true. While the billets are shorter, the cuts are clean compared to the ones made by the saws in the continuous loaders. The saws leave practically all the ends cracked and frayed; they look like paintbrushes.

Rocks in a field are a hazard to machines. For the hand-cutter, striking a rock means a dull blade. Also, the harvester runs down every row, whereas the continuous loader only travels every fourth.

Except in a few places, the machines work all but exclusively on the sand. The exception has been the Talisman Sugar Company, which has been harvesting by machine on the muck since 1972, when their truck drivers struck and the mill was picketed by the United Farm Workers. The next season Talisman replaced all its cutters with machines; they are said to replant every three years.

Some growers keep machines ready to cover lapses in production on the part of the cutters (their performance declines in the heat, for example), or to replace them should they strike. In the past, one grower who did no mechanical harvesting kept a harvester parked in view of the barracks.

To a grower the appeal of mechanical harvesting is the chance to bank money. The costs of his farm—taxes, fertilizer, seed costs, payroll, food for the cutters, equipment and maintenance—he has reduced as much as he can and now they are fixed. He must raise crops that bear abundantly and be rich in sucrose; if, at the end of the season, he harvests thirty tons an acre, he is subtracting costs from less than if he had grown seventy. The only place to shave costs is from the expense of the harvest. The hand-cutters are already laboring at peak efficiency. Savings there can be had only by falsifying the hours the cutters spend in the fields. The concerns of a grower using machines are whether or not he is delivering to the mill cane that will return enough money to have made the shift from hand-cutting worthwhile, and whether or not he is damaging his fields. The first he can know right away. The second will take watching his fields a few years to determine; the greatest decline, with machine-harvested fields, is from the first stubble crop to the second. If savings are high enough, a grower can tolerate the loss of tons in the field.

The special difficulty of developing a harvester for the Florida fields was solving the problem of how to stand up the cane for cutting without pulling the plant from the soil. The problem was solved (in West Germany and Australia) by increasing the width of the harvesters' mouths to five feet, the same width, that is, as the rows; the force of the pull then on the roots was all but eliminated. What held up for years the development of such a machine was that research had concentrated on designing a harvester that would pick up lodged—that is, fallen over—cane, cut it, then lay it back down for the continuous loader.

A signal element of the harvest by machine is the driver. In order for the fields to be cut properly, the blades of the machine must be sharp and the speed at which the harvester proceeds must be coordinated with the speed of the blades. A harvester driven too fast will tear the cane. A dull blade will cut raggedly, leaving the stalk vulnerable to bacteria. To the growers' complaints of damage to the fields, men with an interest in the success of mechanical harvesting say that the damage is the result of poor harvesting practices and that a machine driven properly should do no more harm to a field than a hand-cutter.

There is resistance to the idea of mechanical harvesting. An industry-wide conversion to machines might require a new kind of cane, one that grows fewer suckers, has a stronger root system, stands upright, ratoons well, and doesn't flower, in addition to delivering high levels of sucrose and bearing abundantly. A number of growers feel they have tried mechanical harvesting in the past and were disappointed. Many own machines from various moments of design. There are harvesters parked on the lot at the U.S. Sugar mill in Clewiston. They are huge and lumbering and look as if they were intended for work at the bottom of the sea, or on the surface of the moon. Vines and flowers climb them. The growers feel that no matter how badly a West Indian cuts, he doesn't tear up a field. If the government went out of the business of protecting the price of sugar and the price fell too low, or if there were a crippling strike, or if the industry had too much trouble with lawsuits on behalf of the cutters, hand-cutting might become a luxury.

13

The price that the growers receive for their sugar is protected by quotas on imports. Many people believe that government support of sugar prices is not in the interests of the rest of the country. Denying our market to sugar from the Caribbean, as well as from the Philippines and from Central America, only makes it harder for people in those places to make a living, which difficulty is addressed in the form of American aid sent to replace money that might have been made selling sugar in America. Moreover, excluding sugar from Central America and the Caribbean encourages farmers there to grow drug crops. Also, it encourages countries like the Dominican Republic, the largest exporter of sugar to America and one which has seen its quotas cut almost by half in the last two years alone, to sell sugar to the Soviet Union, which is glad of more trade in the Caribbean. Since 1981 imports of sugar have dropped from five million tons a year to one million, which has made a lot of Americans former workers at sugar refineries. It is possible that the government support of sugar prices costs Americans three billion dollars a year in the form of higher prices for candy bars and ice cream and salad dressings and canned soups and vegetables and cereals and all the other products that contain sugar. If a percentage of the cost of foreign aid were figured in, the amount would be higher. The sugar lobby represents two thousand growers of sugar cane and ten thousand growers of sugar beets. The reason it is so powerful is that it has come to have a fortuitous alliance with the National Corn Growers Association. In 1984 Coca-Cola, the largest consumer of sugar, began using only high-fructose corn syrup. Corn growers now had an interest in seeing that the price of sugar remained as high as possible; they set the price of corn syrup just below it. A congressman from the Northeast has said that the growers of sugar cane and sugar beets and the growers of corn have together organized Congress almost as effectively as has the National Rifle Association.

14

An old man in Belle Glade: "I come into the Glades from Tennessee on December 1, 1942. I had signed up at the House of Customs, which they had a House of Customs back in those days. I got here on a Sunday. They wanted to bring us in open trucks from Memphis, as if this was cattle, but they must have changed their minds because we come on a bus. They had a receiving station and they had a doctor there, same as they do in the army for an exam. I had a brother to come with me, but he wasn't in good enough shape for the exam, so he went back. Tuesday they mustered me out to the Bare Branch camp under a man named McLeod. He had Ritta and Bare Branch camps. He treated people like they were dogs.

"I had heard about the cane offhandedly. There were a lot of what we called man-catchers out there to hustle labor for this or that work, in all fields, not just sugar cane—the highways, the railroads, the turpentine—and they had got people I knew of, signed them up and brought them to the cane fields, so I knew the work was there, but I didn't know exactly what it was. I hadn't talked to nobody who'd come home from it. In back times the companies paid off once a month. I only come down to make a couple of paydays, three or four. But I never did meet the payday. I left the first or second Saturday in January.

"What happened to get me out of it, I started writing letters. First letter I writ from here I wrote to Chief Justice Hughes, he was the head of the Department of Justice; I was writing him because they had 'U.S.' on the signs for the company. He answered my letter in six days. Said he got the letter I wrote him and the way he explained it to me, the company was a subsidiary of General Motors, and the subsidiary had been sold to a subsidiary. Now I don't know, but that's what he wrote me. Then I wrote to the people in the Customs House that sent me there. They said the big fish was paying the little fish to misuse us and there wasn't anything I could do about it. They were using slavery and every other kind of thing else. After that I kept my mouth shut and used every chance I had to escape.

"I cut sugar cane around twenty-one, twenty-two days—that is, I worked *hard* for twenty-one days where I learned about the roughness of cane, and after that no more sugar cane for me. Christmas Day I made a plan to run away. I worked about sixteen more days, left, and when I stopped running I was in South Bay. If I had knew there was cane in South Bay, I wouldn't have stopped then. I run into two mens from a labor camp and I got work there picking beans.

Didn't tell nobody who I was or where I'd come from. Kept my head *down.* I was determined not to get caught, because I knew if you run away they comed and get you and chained you to the bed at night. I saw people locked to the beds. I didn't only see that, I saw some men get a beating. They whopped you with a cane knife. Come around with a cane knife and a sap. Beat and bruised you. It wasn't no freedom, it was worse than the pen. If you had brought a wife, or a ladyfriend, and you weren't no good help, they would take your lady and give her to someone else to sleep with. If you didn't dance to the superintendent's music, they took her."

15

Several nationalities are at work in the fields. In addition to the West Indians and Haitians and Mexicans, there are Australians. Most Mexicans work at planting, but a number drive harvesters or tractors for Sugarland Harvesting, the coop begun by Joe Marlin Hilliard. The Mexicans come mainly from the Rio Grande Valley. Most of them live in the trailer park in Clewiston. When the season is over they drive to Louisiana for strawberries, then Tennessee for strawberries, then Minnesota for sugar beets, then Indiana for tomatoes, then Ohio for pickles, then return to Florida for sugar. People who employ them often say that it is hard to persuade the Mexicans to stay on the farm once the harvest is completed. They say the Mexicans get itchy feet. The Mexicans say that this is a misimpression. They say that if they were able to make enough money in one place they would not travel. They do not like the travel, but they say that it was the way they were raised and that they are making their lives the way their fathers made theirs.

The Australians drive harvesters or repair them; Sugarland's machines are Australian. They learn their specialties at technical schools, where a course of study is five years. The specific names of their trades (boilermaker; fitter and turner) suggest the nineteenth century. Some of the Australians are single, some are married to women at home, some bring their wives, and some meet women here whom they marry. The single men live in a bunkhouse on one side of the shop, the men whose wives have come with them live in trailers on the other. The men who have married American women live in town. Unless they've been on a toot the night before and are treating a hangover, the single men often work on their days off, which they prefer to sitting in the bunkhouse doing nothing. Sometimes a man's wife bears a child while he is away and the father buys a keg of beer and sets it down on the floor in the middle of the shop and they all stand around drinking at the end of the day. Sometimes someone says something he might not have said except for the beer, and the party ends in a dispute. One of the Australians when he loses his temper gets in his truck and races around the fields. He has never told anyone why he does this. The others, from the seats of the harvesters or their trucks or where they are in the fields repairing a piece of equipment, see the trail of dust he is raising, and wonder what the hell he is up to.

The Australian man in charge of the other Australians tells any of them coming to this country for the first time to be careful in the local bars. He says that the younger men from the small towns in Australia tend to be like dogs let loose from a leash when they arrive in America. Australian men, he says, are accustomed to drinking and losing their tempers and shouting insults in bars and meaning no harm by it. Americans, he tells them, take dead serious a thing said to them in anger. The Australians, when they get into fights in local bars, tend to resort to head-butting, which is always a surprise in Florida.

Sugarland has its headquarters in a warehouse of corrugated tin set in the fields behind Hilliard's office. It looks like a small airplane hangar. There is a windsock on the roof. Framed by the doors at one end of the building are the fields. One afternoon while I was standing by the shop door watching the field I saw a fox come out of it, about twenty feet away. He was following a scent and not paying attention and working along the edge of the field coming toward me, and when he saw me he looked like he was about to have a heart attack.

At the end of the day, or on days when the rain has thrown the harvest off schedule and nothing is broken that needs to be fixed and there is no work really to be done on the farm, the Australians sometimes sit around in a room of the shop that has Masonite paneling and a collection of hats bearing the emblems of all the fertilizer companies and manufacturers of heavy machinery they deal with, and drink coffee and talk about Australia. Sometimes the subject is flying foxes, big fruit bats with a head like that of a fox. Colonies of them sleep in trees, hanging upside down. They like to creep along the branches. As a result, they get involved in fights and fall off. If the trees are by water, crocodiles gather beneath them.

Australians in the bush know never to swim in any water beneath a colony of flying fox. Another topic is snakes. In back parts of Australia homeowners sometimes catch snakes and release them in their houses to kill rats. The snakes are better than cats because they pursue their prey up into the rafters and crawl spaces. You wouldn't do it, though, if you had children. Once I heard one of them tell about a time when he and his brother stopped by the road to pick up a big python. They put it in the trunk to take home and show off and lost the key. They took out the backseat and tried to pull the snake out, but he kept wrapping himself in the coils of the springs and couldn't be moved. Finally they parked the car under a tree and left the doors open. Three days later the snake came out. The man said, "The hell with driving around in a car with your good clothes on and a snake in the boot."

Of all the men I have met over the years in south Florida I particularly admire two, Allan Quaid and Fisher Ange. Allan was the Australian in charge of Sugarland Harvesting (he now has his own harvest operation) and the man who picked up the snake with his brother. He is in his late forties. He is six-foot-two and has close-set blue eyes, slightly off-center, a long sloping nose, and sideburns to the bottom of his ears. Small lines and creases radiate from the corners of his eyes. He has brown hair. In profile his legs form closing parentheses. He nearly always wears a billed cap, which throws a shadow across his face like a mask. His complexion is permanently flushed from the time he has spent out of doors and there are lines in a diamond pattern, like grid work, crisscrossing the back of his neck. His voice is deep and his speech percussive. "Joe Marlin" he pronounces "Jahmahlin," so that when I was first in Florida and had met Allan but not Joe Marlin I used to think it amazing that one of the growers was an African. He calls himself a hillbilly, by which he means naïve and unsophisticated, but he has worked in four different countries (also Ireland and England), has had a variety of experiences (fisherman, farmer, migrant worker in fruits, cattle driver, heavy machinery operator, crocodile hunter), heads a prosperous harvesting operation, and owns real estate on two continents, so no one else thinks he is. He is married to an American woman named Robyn, who is a consultant to certain growers on crop problems. They have two young daughters. The four of them spend each summer at Allan's cane farm in Queensland, which has a lawn running down toward the Coral Sea. He used hypnosis to quit smoking but says that although he is no longer attached to cigarettes he still craves something, he just doesn't know what it is.

In the past, cutters who were fortunate might have ended up at Click Farm, working for Fisher Ange, Jr., the farm manager, whose father was farm manager before him. In 1986, Click Farm began a two-year trial of mechanical harvesting, which became permanent. There is a certain amount of pain for Fisher in watching the fields he grows torn up by harvesters. Sometimes he passes one that has just been cut and is all rough and sorry looking and thinks, *Look how they scalped that field.*

Click Farm occupies what was once an old slough from the lake. It is near the Okeelanta camp at the old Moore Haven

Mill and the U.S. Sugar camp at Benbow. A dirt road leading to it from the paved county road runs straight for a mile and a half, beside a canal, through the fields. The camp consists of the farm office, three warehouse barracks made of metal, and two trailers. The cutters lived in the barracks and the leadmen and ticket writers in the trailers. Nearby to the west is the shop: several outbuildings and open-sided sheds with tractor tires piled in them and tractors parked for repair. In front of the barracks are borders of red flowers. The houses have poured concrete floors. They are made of aluminum, with slightly peaked roofs; they resemble Monopoly hotels. The view out their windows across the tops of the cane to the levee is about two miles. The view in all other directions is of cane. Out the back door of the barracks, beside the fields, are clothes dryers and clotheslines and a small cinder-block building where the cutters were paid in cash by the ticket writers while a deputy watched and buses waited to take them to town, and in which they sat and told jokes and drank beer and played reggae tapes loud and danced with each other.

Fisher is tall, with red hair that is thinning on top and that he usually covers with a cap or a cowboy hat made of straw. As a child, he says, "I was red-haired and freckle-faced, fire red." He is fifty-two. He has a large frame and big hands. His mouth hardly moves when he talks. His complexion is high-colored. Sitting in the cab of his truck, figuring the row price on a calculator, he wears reading glasses, which give him the look of a scholar. He has a leather belt that says "Fish" on the back with a buckle that says "Sugar" on it. His dog is named Sugar. He wears a braided gold chain around his neck from which hangs a cross, and a gold bracelet on one wrist and a silver watch on the other. On the visor of his Click Farm–issue sky-blue pickup is a button with a pair of hands joined at the palms and the saying, "Life is Fragile, Handle with Prayer." He once sent home a cutter who had threatened him. He thinks now that he might have provoked the man. "You know more when you're young," he says. He occasionally has a backward, inverted, double-talk way of speaking; once I heard him on the phone, planning a vacation, say, "Nothing I need to bring, which I hope there isn't?" Among the other growers he has the reputation of raising an abundance of excellent cane. He is popular with the people who work for him. The cutters called him Mr. Fisher. He oversees the burning of a field as seldom as possible, preferring to assign the job. He dislikes the commotion, plus he has had two heart attacks, the first while burning. "The second I had harvesting," he says. "I knew I was having it and I waited until my crew was out of the fields, then I went back to the office and said I was having a heart attack and they all laughed at me because I was just standing there, but I went to the hospital and they said, 'Yup, he's having a heart attack.' That laid me up about eight weeks. We set up a two-way radio by the side of the bed."

Fisher described Click as the farm of last resort and as the last stop on the way home to Jamaica, because so many discontented cutters were shipped there from larger growers and then settled down. He says he was never certain whether to take this as a compliment.

Until Click Farm switched to mechanical harvesting, and even for a while after, Fisher regularly received a letter or a card from one cutter or another who had worked for him but had not received a request to come back. A number would arrive around Valentine's Day. A typical one had on its cover a drawing of a chipmunk, holding a strawberry wrapped in a bow, standing beside a bush from which a heart was hanging. The background was pink and above the chipmunk was printed in black, "A Valentine from Your Secret Pal. Can you keep a secret? . . ." And inside: ". . . so can I! Happy Valentine's Day From Guess Who?" Under that was written "To Mr. Fisher from Samuel Forster with lot of love." The note enclosed, from Spring Ground District, Spaulding P.O., Clarendon, West Indies, said,

> Hello Mr. Fisher
> Good day to you and your family and let hope
> you are all fine. This is my greates priviledge
> to writ you this letter. I am longing to hear
> from you so I am asking you please if you
> could give me any information about this
> coming season, I am try my best but I cannot
> make it out hear things are very rough. May
> God bless you.

For five years, beginning in 1958, when he got out of the service, Fisher lived in Ft. Myers, on the coast. He found a job selling insurance and had no intention of returning to the Glades, but then the Cuban Revolution took place, opening up lots of new land to sugar cane, and he grew tired of his life as a salesman. "It's hard to sell an idea," he says. "Whenever you go to sell a person on an idea, you got to start from scratch. If you go to sell him a car, a man's already got his mind made up he wants a car, you just have to sell him the type." Otherwise, nearly all the events of his life have taken place on a landscape enclosed by Moore Haven, Clewiston, the shore of the lake, and the borders of the fields he has care of.

With Fisher: "This is the Benbow camp, and this is where I was born, right here where this open space is by these banana trees. I wasn't born in a hospital. I lived in this camp from 1937 to 1947, first ten years of my life. My father had come from Arcadia, which is a citrus and cattle town about ninety miles from here, between here and Sarasota on the west coast, to work for the Southern Sugar Corporation when the owner was a man by the name of John Gramblin, and apparently the mill went bust and some people who had been with General Motors picked up the old Southern Sugar mill and called it USSC. My daddy went to work for them as a mechanic repairing tractors, but he only did that a few months, then they made him foreman. I don't think they had much more at the time than about four hundred acres, and this was one of the first camps here. My dad worked for the Sugar Corporation eighteen years, then quit and went to work for a man named Moore, who was the vice president of the Stokely Van Camp Canneries out of Knoxville, Tennessee—you still see their products on the shelf all the time, at least in the South, I don't know about anywhere else. He worked for them from 1947 to 1952 being farm manager on a hundred-and-sixty-acre farm growing and harvesting sugar. They loaded about six or seven railroad cars a day back then. We lived at Moore farm, then we moved down the road to

Click Farm; my dad didn't change his occupation any, just changed farms. He was there '52 to '74, working for Click, and I started working for Sugarcane Harvesters—four farms that had been harvesting separately: Roger Weekes, Moore Farm, Friarson Farms, and Click Farms—they incorporated in 1963 and hired me as their manager and I have been here ever since. I got one retired sister that worked for Pan American for thirty years, second sister's a nurse, and then I've got a younger brother in Labelle and he's a farmer, vegetables. My brother and my sisters all have college educations. I'm the only one that didn't get one.

"I had an exciting youth, it just doesn't sound exciting. Till I was five years old I didn't know there was anybody else but a black boy around because that's who I played with. We chased rabbits when the men burned the cane fields—mainly those fields right over there up by the levee—hit them with cane stalks. You'd go home with a string of rabbits and your mother would cook them up. Smother them with gravy and white rice and that was really a specialty. I could stand some of that right now. How we got around is rode horses. In those days growers would cut the cane with domestic help. They would take a train through the South—Georgia, Alabama, North Carolina, South Carolina, some from Virginia—and they'd go out and try and recruit cutters, say, 'Down in Florida we're cutting sugar cane,' and get them down here. You have to understand that in those days they were not far from slavery in south Florida and a white man was something to be feared. You brought these people down here and they didn't particularly like the work, but you'd have to do what you had to to keep a work force here, anything short of violence, I guess. Like a man wants to go home, it wasn't as easy as it is today to get transportation. You just didn't get him transportation, or you would tell him he could go home tomorrow. Whatever you had to do to get him one more day in the field. If you want to use your imagination, there were some tough white people down here in those days. The people who did the harvest were bad too. A lot were fugitives or wanted in some other state. Dad always carried a pair of brass knuckles in his back pocket and that was protection against a man with a cane knife. So that was basically the rules of the road, they'd bring a man in and tell him what was expected of him and assign him a barracks and make him part of a team, cutters and loader, and they would cut cane or load a wagon and the cane was transported to the siding, and at the end of the day they had a blackboard on the wall of the commissary that would say crew number one loaded how much cane and that equaled *x* amount of dollars. If you had any problems, that's where it was, on those steps. If you had any confrontations brewing with anyone, that's where you were going to meet up with it; many times there was physical violence, hand to hand. My daddy used whatever means necessary to carry out his responsibilities, force if he had to, but that's not the way he preferred to go. Back then the foreman had the advantage because they were dominant, so mostly it was a matter of talk and debate. You didn't get much resistance out of anybody. Today there's more recourse for the cutters, they have legal service. Anyway, while these people were out recruiting they'd bring back livestock, horses to replace their own, and my daddy would bring me back a Shetland pony, so I had my own transportation, and I guess I did physically use the camp to reenact whatever cowboy movie I had seen the week before, use the commissary, which was over there where you see those cottages, as the old saloon, and do that all week. I'd tie my horse up outside the commissary and walk in and say, 'Roy, give me a Coke.' I'd be using the sugar estate as a western town. And Roy would say, 'I don't have permission from your daddy to give you a Coke.' So I'd go outside and get a scrap of paper and scrawl something on it, I didn't know how to write yet, and walk back in and hand it to him and say, 'Roy, Daddy give me a note to get a Coke,' and he'd say, 'Well, all right.'

"My dad was in charge of all the camps from here to Clewiston. They cut green cane then. The schoolhouse was the church and the place for the Saturday night dance. My daddy had to be like a deputy sheriff. Saturday night brought the shootouts and the cutups and the fistfights, and Sunday morning brought church, and Monday brought work. You didn't think anything about taking care of domestic problems. I saw my daddy come home one time all bloody and he had over two hundred holes in his shirt, and it was from a woman. She and her husband had been having a domestic fight in the saloon in the camp and my dad was sent in to break it up—Dad acted as his own policeman—and he was having a tussle, actually a fistfight, with her husband and the woman got mad, and she jumped on his back, and she had this little old pocket knife, just with about a quarter-inch blade, and she started sticking him in the back, just peppering his back. It was rough. Everybody there was tough—not me, but my daddy and the people his age were.

"If you worked for the company and you weren't sick, you were supposed to be on the job. I was with my dad one time, this is maybe 1939 or '40, I guess I was three or four, and as I said everyone used to get by the blackboard at the commissary, and this one big black guy, about six-foot-four and huge—my dad was six-foot-three and weighed about two-twenty, and this guy made my dad look like a dwarf—anyhow this one guy had been laying up about four or five days for no good reason, and he knew so, and he met my dad that afternoon when he came in from the fields and dad got out of the truck and started to walk to the time office, which was beside the commissary, and this guy was on the porch and there were about ten or twelve other people there, and the guy says, 'Well Mr. Fisher, I guess you noticed I ain't been at work these last few days.' This guy went on talking, and all the time he was talking my dad was getting on those brass knucks. After a while of talking this guy couldn't stand it, baiting my father, he had to see how the people behind him were taking it, and when he turned to see what they were thinking, about how they were taking his talking back to the bossman, he turned his head about forty-five degrees, and my dad clocked him behind the right ear and he went down. Frazier and Sweet—they were called yard men, but they were really just troubleshooters, bodyguards, I guess you could say, their job was to back my daddy up—anyway, Frazier and Sweet helped my dad pick the man up and load him in the truck. My dad drove him into town to the doctor, and the doctor looked at him and told my dad the man was okay, and my daddy said, 'This man has given me a hard time and I need for you to keep him a couple of days so that he can be a kind of example.' So the doctor smiled and said, 'All right, Mr. Ange, I'll keep him here.' A couple of days later he called and said, 'You can pick up that man now,' and when my dad saw him the man had lost six or eight pounds and my dad said, 'What happened?' and the doctor said, 'We had him on a little soup and castor oil diet.' It probably didn't hurt the man none, but it impressed on him how bad that encounter was. I guess Dad kind of got his respect around the back door. Up until then all I had seen was an imaginary world which was the camp that I lived in. The only time I encountered the real world was that time. I shouldn't have been there, and if my daddy had known he was going to have trouble, I wouldn't have been there."

16

$: The means for determining how cutters are paid are secret and complex and deliberately obscured by the growers. It is known that a grower assigns to a cut row a value called the row price and that a cutter is paid by the portion of the row he completes. That is, a cutter finishing half of a cut row worth forty dollars earns twenty. Regardless of the value of the row, agreements made between the growers and the Department of Labor guarantee cutters an hourly wage. This figure is called the Adverse Effect Wage Rate and is designed to protect wages in an area from the consequences of importing workers.

Growers began not long ago to claim that they pay strictly by means of a measure called a task rate. Previously they said in their contracts that rates of pay would be determined by means of either a piece rate or a task rate. Some growers mentioned only piece rate, others mentioned both. Those using both (none used only task rate) made no distinction between them. In 1983, a district court in Washington, D.C., laid out guidelines for employers paying according to piece rates. Among other things, the decision meant that employers using them would have to follow rules set by the Department of Labor and would be liable to having their pay practices monitored by the Department in order for the government to be sure the employers were complying. The next year, growers who had used "piece rate" in their contracts deleted the phrase, substituting "task rate." The industry claimed that since they were paying by a task rate they were not subject to piece rate standards imposed by the Department of Labor. The Department allowed them to do so.

Various lawsuits brought lately on behalf of the cutters have forced growers to reveal a little about their methods of payment. Insofar as they are willing to be specific about how they pay cutters, the growers contend (in affidavits filed with the Department of Labor) that this is their formula for determining the value of a row:

> *Adverse Effect Wage Rate × the hours required for the row to be cut by less productive workers = row price.*

The determination of how many hours a row will require is the result, they say, of expert attention to the abilities of the cutters and the conditions of the fields. The misrepresentation this answer involves is arrived at by inverting certain aspects of the truth and is not unresourceful.

Cutters are in fact paid by means of a piece rate, the increment of payment being the ton. The actual formula for assigning value to a row begins with an estimate of how many tons the field it is part of contains. The grower derives from this figure the number of tons to a row. This amount he doubles to arrive at the number of tons to the cut row. The new figure he multiplies by the price per ton he has budgeted for harvest. Thus a forty-ton field with, say (for the sake of simplicity), four tons to the row, eight to the cut row, times, say, three dollars and fifty cents a ton for harvest (a figure used by a grower in 1986–1987), gives a row price of twenty-eight dollars.

Certain factors may cause the grower to revise this figure before issuing it. An insufficient burn leaves a field more difficult to cut. A thicker row is more work. Cane fallen over and tangled is harder to manage. A knife cutting cane with a stalk of high fiber or cutting in a field full of rocks must be sharpened more often. Work performed on a day following heavy rain, when the field is muddy and has water standing in it, proceeds slowly. If the grower wants to speed it up, he may increase the price.

A supervisor pricing a field is likely to visit it after the burn. If he is still uncertain over the estimate he may talk to people who have worked closely on the field. He may go out first thing in the morning, in the dark, and circle it. He may walk into it and cut a few stalks and lay them in the truck bed and measure them. Or multiply the number of stalks in a stool by their heights; a stool containing eight stalks five feet high gives a forty-ton field.

. . .

A variation on the row price is paid for rows beside a canal or a road or at the edge of a field. These are called Charlie Frank rows; no one knows why, or whether it is a Jamaican or American term. It has been in use for years. Charlie Frank rows bear more heavily because they receive more light. Being on the outside of the field they also burn less completely. Since the Charlie Frank rows are harder to cut and also require that the man cutting them drag his cane across to the pile of the man working beside him, they pay the most in the field. Exactly how much depends on the policy of the grower. Some growers pay ten per cent more, some fifteen or twenty, and some pay a flat fee above the price of the rest of the rows in the field. If the field contains an even number of rows, the cutter will harvest the Charlie Frank row and the row beside it. In a field where the rows amount to an odd number, he will cut only the Charlie Frank row and be paid the price of a cut row. Next to Charlie Frank is the coochie row. The Jamaicans say: It sister to Charlie Frank and it have a lot of cane, but it pay no more.

The row price is also amended to pay for a throwover row. A throwover row is any row where a cutter has to throw his cane across one row in order to pile it. Cutters call it a trover row. A grower uses a throwover row down the middle of a field, or to one side or the other of the middle, to open a route for the continuous loader in order not to have it drive over the piles of cane. Some growers feel the loader does no damage to the cane in passing over it and don't want to pay extra for the throwover row and so do without it. The throwover row is also a certain row in a field with an odd number of rows and without a Charlie Frank row, or a row beside a ditch bank, because the loader needs ten feet of clearance from a ditch. A field with an even number of rows must have two throwover rows, if it has any at all. The throwover row pays the same as a Charlie Frank row. In addition, if a grower has sent a tractor down a row to make a firebreak, he will pay extra for that row to be cut, usually ten per cent. If that row happens to be a Charlie Frank row, it will customarily pay twenty per cent above the row price of the field.

Cane fields are mainly laid out on the grid, except here and there where the shape of the land prevents it. A common variation is a field in the shape of a triangle. Each row then is priced at a portion of the longest row or else by the foot. Cutters call this kind of field a rob angle, because it costs them the chance to make their full money.

A man on a smaller farm might do the arithmetic of the row price in his head, or with a calculator. Larger growers supply their supervisors with charts on which are written numbers of tons with corresponding prices. Some growers supply two rates, one for a field with no complications and one which includes a bonus to be applied in consideration of the conditions of the field. Growers whose charts have no bonus rate take the variables of the field into account by other means. They consider a thirty-ton field with a poor burn and tangled cane to be as difficult to cut as, say, a thirty-five-ton field well burned and with straight cane, and apply the price from the heavier field.

Growers commonly overpay at the start of the season. The first fields cut are the oldest on the farm and the ones in worst shape, the burns are less efficient, and the cutters are working themselves into form and need an incentive to improve. What the growers spend at the start of the harvest, they recover as the season progresses. Row prices decline over the course of the harvest. By the end, cutters are working in fields of plant cane, their stamina is greater, their pace quicker, the burns are complete, and what may earlier have looked like a difficult field is something they now easily handle. Prices start high, decline to an average around the middle of the harvest, and fall by the end.

In the beginning of the season an accomplished cutter may earn as much as six or seven dollars an hour. Because the number of tons in the field on which the row price is based is an estimate, the money paid for the harvest of the field may not agree with the row price. If a grower has estimated fewer tons in a field than are there, he has made money on the cutters. If he has estimated more, they have made money on him. "You put a cutter in a twenty-ton field you priced at thirty-five," a grower has said, "and he is going to eat your lunch." How growers are able to hold to their budgets is by reviewing printouts from the mill which tell them the number of tons delivered from a field and the amount of sugar recovered. If they discover they paid more for a field than they intended, they make adjustments on another to get it back. What they lose on one field they recover on another. Some keep in mind fields they know will be easy to cut and hold them in reserve for a time when they need to get back some money. "When you get to a straight field," a grower has said, "you try to get back the three to four per cent extra you paid for the tangled field." Some growers keep strictly to their price per ton figure and adjust their row prices daily, others stay as close to the figure as they can and shave here and there and check every week or two, or once a month, or every quarter of the season to see how they are doing.

Some growers keep dropping their prices until someone, perhaps a leadman, comes to them and says the cutters are talking about a strike. Occasionally when a cutter enters a field he will call out, "What a row?" but usually they don't ask the price. They are concerned that if trouble develops over money they might be identified as having begun it.

Some growers, usually the smaller ones, in the interests of camp harmony, will return to the cutters on one field the money they made off them on another. On the occasions when they are giving money back they want the cutters to know it. What they usually do is visit the field and make an announcement. They will practically rent a brass band. Some growers will immediately correct a price if their cutters dispute it. They manage in this way to maintain the respect of their cutters, which they hope means they will get their cutters' best work, which is capital to draw on during periods of pressure. During training some growers tell the men that they will not change a price once they make it. They say they might adjust it later on another field, but they won't change it for the field the cutters are in. "If you let them see that you might be a double-minded person," a grower told me, "they'll really get to you."

Two growers would not price a field the same, because each has budgeted a different figure per ton, which introduces an inequity: cutters have no say over where they are assigned; those who end up with growers whose price per ton figure is higher have already gained an advantage over the others.

How growers are able to be specific about the length of time a cutter will take to complete a row is by knowing exactly how many tons the cutter must harvest per hour in order to earn the Adverse Effect Wage Rate. This figure they derive by dividing their per-ton harvest figure into the Rate. The grower budgeting three dollars and seventy-five cents a ton when the Rate is five-thirty knows that his cutters must account for 1.41 tons an hour for the grower to stay on his harvest budget. From this figure growers can also determine how many feet a cutter must cover in an hour, depending on the tonnage of the field. Some growers include this information on their charts. These distances are the production tasks the cutters must match in order to hold on to their jobs. Some growers measure off this distance in the field and mark it with a flag; pushers can then keep an eye on the progress of the cutters and urge ahead those who are lagging.

A cutter whose earnings fall short of the Adverse Effect Wage Rate is entitled to the difference between it and what his effort has brought him. This difference is called build-up. A cutter drawing build-up too regularly is likely to be fired. After the first of the year most cutters are accomplished enough that few of them draw build-up. Those who do are usually coming back from an injury.

It has been the practice of some growers to credit a cutter with fewer hours in the field than he has worked. Their ticket writers are instructed to divide the row price by the Adverse Effect Wage Rate and issue the corresponding hours, which saves the growers a lot of money. Growers operating in this fashion can set row prices at levels so low that many cutters are unable to make the minimum rate; the grower then evades paying build-up by having his ticket writers doctor the hours. A man who takes eight hours to cut a thirty-six-dollar row is owed money by the grower. If the ticket writer reports that he cut it in six, the debt is erased. This practice is called matching hours, or shaving hours, or cooking hours. Cutters who exceed the task are issued extra hours, in order not to throw off the scale. An accomplished cutter I know routinely receives nine and nine and a half hours on days when he has only cut for six.

In Jamaica, at his house on top of a mountain, in the rain, I interviewed a man who, until he was not rehired for the harvest beginning in the fall of 1987 (he doesn't know why), had been a ticket writer for Okeelanta for seven seasons and a cutter for ten before that. He said that ticket writers refer to the process of matching hours to pay as balancing. How they knew to do it, he said, was that every ten days, or every fortnight, the ticket writers would be summoned to a meeting at which they were not allowed to speak or ask questions and at which a supervisor would tell them that the amount of build-up the company was paying would have to be cut. He said the ticket writers were never told to shave the hours but that it was understood among them that that was the intention of the meeting. It was also understood that ticket writers who did not cooperate would be put back on the knife or sent home. He also said that when a man had fallen behind from sickness or fatigue or bad luck he would try to give him as many hours as he could without getting in trouble with the company, which practice, he said, was known among ticket writers as squeezing the hours.

A famous document in the recent history of sugar cane

harvesting is the Sugarman Report. Solomon Sugarman was a wage and hour analyst with the Department of Labor when he came to Florida in 1973 to examine the wages and record-keeping practices of the sugar cane industry. The Department of Labor was interested to know whether the proper wage was being paid to the cutters and whether the hours reported for the piece work were accurate.

Sugarman and his crew stayed four days and visited four growers: Atlantic Sugar Association, Sugar Cane Growers Cooperative, United States Sugar Corporation, and Gulf + Western Food Products Company, which has since sold its interests to a family from Cuba named Fanjul. Sugarman selected these growers because among them they employed three-quarters of the cutters. At two companies (U.S. Sugar and Sugar Cane Growers Cooperative) he found that cutters were counted as having begun work half an hour after getting off the bus, were docked half an hour for lunch whether they took it or not (Sugarman noticed that if the cutters took lunch breaks at all they were no longer than fifteen minutes and usually amounted to five), and had their quitting times rounded back to the last full hour they were seen in the field—that is, a cutter quitting at three-fifty-five was said to have stopped at three o'clock. He decided that this cost the cutters an hour and a half a day (although in order to avoid charges of unfairness in his minimum-wage study, he reduced this figure to one hour). At one company (Atlantic), he found that the ticket writers recorded whatever hours were necessary to satisfy the minimum-wage requirements. The day Sugarman was there, Atlantic recorded cutters' hours in half-hour increments. Reviewing the master payroll list, Sugarman found that none of the increments had been entered. He also discovered in checking past records that ticket writers had recorded the increments that day only, leading him to conclude that this had been done on instructions from the company, because of the survey. While he and his team were in the field watching a row being cut, word came from the offices that the row price was to be raised to thirty dollars, from twenty-four. Sugarman concluded that the company had instructed its timekeepers to record hours accurately as long as Sugarman was around, then had realized that this would show that they weren't paying the minimum wage, so had hustled out to the field. Sugarman learned from the company's records that Atlantic generally paid row prices of twenty, twenty-three, twenty-four, and twenty-six dollars. At Sugar Cane Growers Cooperative he found that hours were issued on the basis of satisfaction of the task; every person cutting a quarter row, that is, received the same number of hours. When I called to ask about the survey, he told me that at one company, which he wouldn't name, he had found three ticket writers asleep on a bus.

Sugarman's findings regarding the minimum wage (he discovered violations at all companies except Gulf + Western) were eventually discredited by the industry. The regulations the growers were expected to satisfy in terms of pay were to be met over the course of a fortnight, and Sugarman's visit of four days was not long enough to be conclusive. The incontrovertible value of Sugarman's study was that it documented the shaving of hours. An irony of the report is that no violations were discovered at Gulf + Western. Under the Fanjul family the company, of all growers, has been the most consistently criticized by cutters for the stealing of hours.

17

Caveman had the idea that we might find his friend from Barbados in a bar in Harlem, so we parked one afternoon in a gravel lot outside a low brick building with a flat roof and no windows and walked past two guys leaning against a car who stared hard at me (later I learned from Caveman that they had concluded I was a cop), and I followed him through the door and when my eyes adjusted I could see that there were two pool tables in front of me and a small dance floor and a sign on the wall that said "Positively No Gambling Allowed At Pool Tables Or In Rest Rooms" and across the room a bar with a mirror behind it reflecting all the liquor bottles, and the faces of the men at the bar, and the back of a tall, stately woman handing over set-ups and filling plastic cups almost to the top with liquor. Caveman went up to a man leaning on the bar and tapped his shoulder. The man turned around and Caveman said something and I think the man must have misunderstood because he said, "How much are you paying?" Caveman shook his head and found another man at the end of the bar. The first man followed him, asking how much work there was, and Caveman had to wave him off. After he had said a few words to the other man, Caveman turned to me and said, "Here." The man was clearly an American and not from Barbados. He said that he had cut cane about fifteen years ago, but wouldn't do it no more. He said he had been a fast cutter and had made some money. While Caveman watched the pool players, the man talked, but it was hard for me to hear because of the noise in the bar and because he kept lowering his head and speaking to the floor. The only part I made out clearly was when he looked at me and said, "And I'll tell you one more thing. . . ." After I had been listening to him for a couple of minutes, I became aware that a somber-looking young man wearing dark clothes, a felt hat, and a black leather jacket was watching me from a few feet away. In a moment he came up and said, "When you finish I want to talk to you," then he walked away; I didn't see where. The man I had been listening to asked if I had any more questions and I said I didn't and he went back to the bar. Caveman and I left. On the way to the car the guy who had said he wanted to talk to me stepped up and blocked my way. He said, "You want to read a master's thesis I wrote on the Vital Link?" Caveman grabbed my arm and said, "Let's get out of here." In the car he said that the man who had just spoken to me had a good education but was a rockhead, a junkie. Caveman asked if I had understood the man in the bar, and I said that I hadn't. Caveman said, "Well, now, he was telling you something."

18

Compared to other crops, varieties of sugar cane have pedestrian names. CP 75-1553 is one, and CP-78-2114 is another. In the past, when there were fewer kinds, there was a variety called yellow gal, because it had a yellow stalk, and one called purple ribbon and one called yellow ribbon, because they had bands of those colors at their joints. There was a variety that was best harvested the week before and the week after Christmas, and this was called Christmas cane. There is a cane called grind down cane, which does not refer to any specific variety. It is cane that is said to mature two weeks after it has been ground, as in, "You sure would have got some sucrose if you'd waited another two weeks."

Approximately fifty varieties of sugar cane are available to the growers. Some have been popular in the past and are now in decline and some never quite worked out. Seven are in widespread use: two are not very good on cold land—that is, land more susceptible to frost—four account for most of the acreage, and one accounts for more than half.

The two most desirable attributes are high sucrose and high tonnage. The pair must accompany each other; high tonnage alone will break a grower in harvest costs. In addition, the mills like cane of low fiber since it is more easily handled. Growers like cane that is resistant to disease and that ratoons well; they despise a poor stubbler.

Although most growers favor one variety over the others, none plants only one. To satisfy the schedule of the mill, they must design their farms to include varieties that mature at the beginning, the middle, and the end of the harvest. Also, they must plan against an attack of disease; different varieties have different qualities of resistance. Furthermore, the farms are large enough that many are likely to include different conditions of soil. Land quality decreases as one travels farther from the lake. Growers close to the lake plant one kind of cane, those farther away another. Some growers test cane for the industry, or try long shots on what they call a here, there, and yonder basis.

Sugar cane breeds are developed at Canal Point, on the east side of the lake, by the United States Department of Agriculture, and at Clewiston by U.S. Sugar. Two of the four breeds which are popular were developed at Clewiston and two at Canal Point. Canal Point is the older institution. It was brought into being to create varieties for the Louisiana industry.

"Breeding sugar cane is not that simple." (This is Dr. Joseph Orsinigo, botanist at the Florida Sugar Cane League.)

"Genetically, there is tremendous variation. Sugar cane is *Saccharum officianarum*, but what we grow commercially are two- and three-part hybrids of *robustum*, *spontaneum*, and *officianarum*. We develop new varieties by making crosses from a parent stock. It's hard work. It's field work. Let's say we plant sixty thousand seedlings—that's not an unusual number. We lose half to disease. The rest: some are weak, they blow over, you might lose a few to rabbits, rats, and pigs. From sixty thousand we may end up with twelve hundred at the end of one year, and from that we end up with three hundred the following year. We select then as many as twelve and plant each on nine farms under eight conditions of soil and climate, what are called field trials. From these plots, over three years, we get a plant crop and two ratoon crops. By the second year you pretty well know whether or not a variety will be suitable for industrial use. Many years you get none. In the final year of testing, the cane is inoculated as well as can be against all disease. At the end of the trials I plant it. The next year I increase the planting, the following year I increase the increase. That crop is then increased for sale. We send a letter to the growers telling them a new variety is available and enclose a list of its characteristics and performance. The growers who made land available for the trials get first crack at the new cane, at a discounted price. They also have a good idea of how the new variety will do on their land.

"This year we have two varieties for sale: CP 75-1553 and CP 78-2114. CP means they were developed at Canal Point; Clewiston cane is CL. 75 and 78 tell the year of their selection as trials, and 1553 and 2114 indicate the rows they were taken from. CP 78-2114 was first put on the market in 1986.

Eight years is quick for a cane to be selected. Usually it takes ten.

"Now, among varieties characteristics are variable. One might be that the variety produces a higher tonnage of cane, or more sucrose in the juice, or it may be able to germinate or grow better on wet land, or have a slightly better resistance to cold. It may stubble better. The variety that is planted on most of the acres is a variety that does not germinate or grow rapidly under wet conditions or cold, so if a grower planted that next to the old industry standard and experienced rain or cold he would question whether he had made a big mistake.

"There are varieties that will grow erect in the muck but deliver about thirty tons to the acre, and the grower wants more. Some cane grows straight but bends after burning and forms a mat, the growers won't work it, and that is replaced by a variety that ratoons well but produces less tonnage. And that is replaced by one that might produce a high tonnage but not as much juice.

"What we don't need is an average dog. We need winners by site. We are trying to give an offering that will satisfy our growers on their own farms. It's unreasonable to expect that one variety will work for the entire area. We had one cane that was a winner on farms close to Lake Okeechobee—that is, it did well on a tight soil, one that's difficult to water, a warm location, frost protected. The cane produced high tonnage, it had good juice characteristics, but unfortunately it was susceptible to the disease called sugar cane smut. Plus, it could not be grown twenty miles from the lake. Furthermore, you couldn't plant it in cold or wet or from a truck where the wheels might run over it; it was delicate.

"A major criterion is tolerance of cold. We know we will never come up with a variety that will withstand ten hours at twenty-five degrees. That is certain death. Twenty-six in the bud doesn't leave you much hope. Twenty-seven is going to be rough. Twenty-eight or twenty-nine, there'll be some survivors. From December on we are not looking for growth, we want maturity. By the time the first of February arrives we will probably have had temperatures below thirty-two. Cane grows hardly at all in temperatures under seventy degrees. In summer the growth rate is about five eighths of an inch to an inch a day. That's in good light with plenty of water and some heat. It's down to one eighth of an inch by late fall.

"So you want vigor, you want good early growth, you would like to have a large top leaf that shades the soil and reduces weed control problems, you want to plant to tillers—that is, varieties that will ratoon well, send out multiple shoots to have a large number of plants per acre—you want a plant that is resistant to root damage and disease, you would prefer a cane that doesn't flower rapidly because the quality of the juice declines once the flower appears, you want a plant that produces high tonnage per acre, that stands as erect as possible to make it easier to harvest, low in fiber because high fiber causes difficulties in harvesting and milling—the man in the field has to sharpen his knife more often and at the mill more fiber means more steam produced to mill it—a plant that does not have any other chemicals in it or waxes that interfere with the extraction of sucrose, a plant that is cheap to grow, cheap to harvest, and yields a lot.

"It doesn't, by the way, exist."

19

The camp I would drive past at Moore Haven consists of three long, low dormitories like poultry barns, made of metal, with corrugated metal roofs. At night the lights were on inside and the doors were open, and for a second as I passed I could see the rows of beds and the cutters lying on them. I would pass, turn around, pass in the other direction, turn around, pass again. There was time on each pass to notice one thing. A man gesturing in the air before him with his hand. A man laying a card on a table. A man on a bed reading a letter. A man on the phone. A man on his way to the sinks with a toothbrush in his hand. The profiles of two men talking. A figure in the yard watching the night, his arms at his side or folded across his chest, his head turning slowly as he followed my car with his eyes.

I began to meet cutters on my own. It turned out they were crazy about having their pictures taken; they couldn't get enough of it. I would trespass at night at the camps and take their pictures and give them a print. When one man thought another had photographed well, he would tell him, "You catch good." One night after I had taken a couple of rolls I put down my camera and said, "Enough pictures. Now you must tell me about cutting sugar cane." I was sitting among perhaps twenty cutters. I reached into my knapsack for my notebook and when I looked up only one remained, the man on whose bed I was sitting. Through him I met others.

I continued, though, to travel with Caveman, because I felt it was broadening.

20

"At approximately five minutes to five in the morning the lights come on and you leave your dreams." (A cutter.) "Then brushing your teeth, then putting on clothes, then about five-thirty it's time for the mess hall and approximately breakfast lasts twenty-five minutes, and by six o'clock you come back and get yourself ready for work, which leaves about six-thirty, and it starts about seven. It was always said that a slow start makes any job harder, so after we get ourselves beginning to work and the body becomes hot and start to sweat, we just keep on going, because it is an everyday thing for us, so we continue to work and maybe bossman come around and see something that not right and say we should fix it, then we have a water wagon, then time to refile a new edge on our cutting knife, then smoking a cigarette, maybe one or two jokes, somebody may share a joke then somebody else always pick it up, and we make ourselves as one, make a unity among us throughout the field.

"At rice time, about ten o'clock or ten-thirty, the rice truck come around, bring your food. Maybe each man feel within himself that it's going to take too much time from the task, so he don't spend too long having a bite. I drink some petrol, put some more edge on the knife, smoke a cigarette, cut a couple of jokes, then suddenly everything become silent and there is just the chopping sound. Start to concentrate again, that a feeling every man know for himself, because losing concentration, making a wrong move, suddenly you find yourself cut. Each man want to finish his row before the other man, that way when work is available he can cut another piece, maybe even another half. If you finish before Let's Go and you are within walking distance to the camp, maybe you go walk, maybe wait for the bus. You think: *Another day has been completed successfully, without any hurt, or physical injury, or serious damage.*

"Then wash. Then rest. After coming from the field we generally speak about the day. Some guy may say he got stranded someplace, he may have got stuck on a rougher row than I, and maybe he only got about a row and a quarter. Mostly we always talk about the price. We say price is not good enough. Who has got the experience of cutting cane maybe seven or eight seasons, maybe twelve, say maybe price was right. Get some food, drink some petrol, maybe write some letters. Then think about tomorrow. Tomorrow is another workday; we always thinking about tomorrow. You see this cane cutting is dangerous work. Grilling, backbreaking, strenuous, and rough. The bending is tremendous strain on your back, your shoulders twisting left, twisting right, bending up and down, lifting. Every day, every season, some may go through some kind of experience where he knows that he could have been hurt in so many ways, where he narrowly escape. My first year, that was my trying year. I came to get experience of it because I have friends at home that talk about cutting cane in America, and I thought I might like to cut a try. I didn't know much about cane cutting, they told me back home that it was very very hard, rough, the sun burn you like you never been burn before. Well, I was intrigued by such a tale and, being as a young man coming up in the world, I said to myself, I must have that experience. When I got here it was much harder. Hearing is only one thing; actually going into the business is rougher. No one is there to help you and you are on your own. Sometimes I cry, sometimes I couldn't sleep at night. But I have a determination to really do it. I say to myself at night: *I can make it.* The next year wasn't as hard. I make some more money the third year, then more, then each year improves. The roughness I know what it is now. I never have any accident or any real real real sickness that disable me to work. Maybe I stop one, two, three days at most with the flu; when you work sometime the rain come and quit you and you do not reach the bus in time and you find yourself catching the flu. I never want to be absent from work, I want to be there each day. That's my intention, not even to lose one hour, if that's possible.

"Now it's nearing the end of the crop, and each man have the intention that each day completed is another day nearer to home. Each man is thinking about the life he left, making plans, buying necessary things, saving some money, all that. If I was at home now with my friends, the season over, I would say, Imagine, look where I was last month, today the sun is hot, I was out there in a field, today here I am sitting in a cool place, reading a magazine, drinking a cool drink, like in a movie or a novel, and what was I doing on that date, for example, maybe it is the fifteenth of July, to say all right, compare the fifteenth of July with the fifteenth of February, when I was cutting cane and here I am just sitting here looking back into where I came from. And they are making some jokes, thinking about something someone do that make everyone laugh, or calling someone a name that he didn't like and had to accept, because everybody keep calling him by it and he just have to learn to answer and be cool. I would tell them then that back in 1983 I was working and I had about one week left before going home and that time I was feeling good cutting cane because I wanted to make some money, and I think the price of the row was thirty-five dollars, and there was work available for all through the day, and I did my first row early in the morning before rice truck came, and I was way up on the second row, I have about one eighth left on the second row of the whole thirteen hundred feet, and I was going so fast because in completing the second row I would make seventy-five dollars for the day, so I had about one eighth row left, and I make a chop and I go down so hard and I feel something hit me in the right eye, and I had to come back up and I said to myself, *Lord Jesus, I'm blinded now,* and I stop working. I trembling, shaking all over, I didn't know where I was, I was at a loss, so eventually I start to check how serious was my injury, I say to myself there must be blood all over and that eye must be no more in use, and after I say these things I start to imagine all kind of scary things that could happen, nobody would really need me, all one eye, and they would send me home and nothing be waiting for me there. I take my hand, I was dirty from the cane all over, and I had a handkerchief and I wipe off my hands with it, still trembling, though, I put the clean hand where the injury was and after that I feel something sticking out of the corner of my right eye, at the same time it wasn't focusing. I am saying to myself, this eye is of no more use, and after taking out the piece sticking there I say there must be blood covering my face, so I squinting. Still trembling, though, I start to notice I could see through it, and I sit up then ten feet in the air and come down. Still standing. The thing I took out was a piece of cane top about an inch long—it went right in the bottom lid and went right out—and then I put my hands on my head and I close my two eyes and it was like I start to preach, 'You guys over there when you go to your bed at night you should pray, because what has happened to me right now, it's only for the almighty God above that has kept me from blindness!' And they are all dropping their knives to see what was the noise."

21

In the fall of 1941, a number of black men in Mississippi, Tennessee, Arkansas, and Alabama accepted invitations from recruiters or answered ads for work at the United States Sugar Corporation. An advertisement that circulated in Memphis said:

ENJOY FLORIDA SUNSHINE
DURING THE WINTER MONTHS
COLORED FARM WORKERS

Men and Women between ages 18 and 60 years of age.

Can procure steady employment until spring, harvesting Sugar Cane on the Plantations of the UNITED STATES SUGAR CORPORATION, at Azucar and Clewiston Florida.

GOOD WAGES
GOOD LIVING CONDITIONS
FREE TRANSPORTATION AND MEALS
TO FLORIDA

CASH ISSUED EVERY DAY
FREE HOUSE RENT, RECREATION,
AND MEDICAL ATTENTION

APPLY
UNITED STATES EMPLOYMENT SERVICE,
FARM DIVISION

Phone 8-6066 *815 Arkansas St.*
Ask for Mrs. Kitts

Among those in Alabama who responded was Allen Slayton, from Tuscaloosa. A man from the sugar company told Slayton he would make thirty dollars a week in the cane fields. He left Tuscaloosa with other recruits in a truck provided by the company on a Tuesday at two in the afternoon. They were given their first food the next evening. The following night they got more. The next afternoon, they arrived in Clewiston, where they were told they each owed the company eight dollars for the ride. In addition, they were charged seventy-five cents for a blanket, fifty for a cane knife, and thirty for a file. The following morning they were roused at three-thirty, given a small breakfast, and taken to the fields at four-thirty. At eleven-thirty they were given a small meal, then worked until dark. Slayton was paid a dollar-eighty for his first few days, then two dollars for a couple of days, then a dollar-twenty. The water supplied in the field was dirty. For fresh water the cutters paid the company five cents a gallon. They worked every day of the next several weeks. Word passed among them that they would be killed if caught trying to escape, and that if they made it to the road they would be arrested for hitchhiking or for vagrancy and returned to the plantation. Slayton asked the superintendent if he could leave; the superintendent said no. Slayton was bitten on the hands by a snake or a spider and the wound became infected. For four days he asked to see a doctor but was ignored. His hands were swollen and he could not work. Another cutter, trying to treat him, cut open one of his hands, and Slayton was then taken to a doctor. Slayton's sister drove from Tuscaloosa to get him. Slayton asked again if he could leave. The supervisor asked if he planned to leave all this free doctoring behind, then said he could go. Nine other cutters slipped out through one of the fields and joined Slayton and his sister in her car.

Johnnie Gray left Tuscaloosa a few days after Slayton. The man from the sugar company told him that he would not make less than six dollars a day. When Gray arrived he learned he would make a dollar-eighty, and that he owed six dollars for transportation (the company records show he was charged eight), as well as a dollar for a blanket, a dollar for a badge to identify him as an employee of the company, fifty cents for a cane knife, and twenty cents for a file. In Tuscaloosa the company man told him and the other cutters they would be well taken care of on the trip. Forty-three left together on a Thursday afternoon and were given their first food—two pieces of bread and some bologna—the following day. That night they were given three more slices of bread, a slice of bologna, and three oranges each. Work began at three-thirty in the morning and did not finish until eight-thirty at night. When Gray complained to the foreman, the foreman said, "I know you are going to work if you stay here, and I am not worried about you staying here, because I know you can't get away." The white supervisors carried guns and blackjacks; guards with heavy sticks patrolled the fields. Gray was overheard by a supervisor saying that he was going to run away and the supervisor told him that he would be caught and brought back, if he wasn't found dead in a canal.

Andrew Green, also from Tuscaloosa, saw a man beaten by the supervisor. Green and the others were paid once a month. Until they received their checks they were in debt to the company. Meanwhile, they were given small advances to cover their board, which kept them in debt. During his second week at the camp Green and another man asked the supervisor if they could leave and were told they couldn't. One man escaped and was brought back. Green got away by giving a woman he had met a letter to his brother in Tuscaloosa and asking her to mail it for him. The brother drove to Florida and waited at night in his car on the highway and Green slipped away in the dark.

Neil Smith would not buy the blanket the company was selling because the bunks were too filthy. He and eight other men built a fire each night in the yard and slept beside it. He worked thirteen days, then got away by saying that his wife was sick and he was going home to see her and would return with his five sons to the fields. The supervisor was glad to hear this and let him go. Smith received forty cents for thirteen days' work. Mr. Mack, the supervisor, whose real name was McLeod, ran a bar on the plantation where the cutters were allowed to gamble; Mack took a cut from each game. If the cutters gambled anyplace else, Mack arrested them (he was a deputy sheriff) and had them taken to Clewiston where they were each fined twenty-five dollars; the fines they worked off in the fields. Smith saw one man run away only to be caught by Mack and fined forty dollars and put back to work in the field. He and the other cutters were constantly threatened by their supervisors and the guards and told that if they didn't behave, they'd be whipped.

Johnnie Green left Tuscaloosa on a Thursday and arrived in Clewiston Saturday morning at four-thirty. He asked to be sent to the South Shore camp, where his brothers were. When he arrived they were surprised to see him and asked what he was doing there, since, by their judgment, the camp was next thing to prison. He got scared and ran off his first night and went back to Tuscaloosa, then came back in a car and got word to his brothers that he was waiting for them. Nine men altogether slipped out through the fields and went back with him to Alabama.

A man named Long wrote his mother from Clewiston saying that the food was very poor, the accommodations were poor, and the place he was living was worse than any prison in the world. He had left Tuscaloosa on a Wednesday afternoon and got no food until Thursday morning, when he was given half a loaf of bread and a can of beans. At midnight on Thursday, at Tampa, the truck he was traveling in stopped by a store and he was given ten cents and told to get whatever he wanted. He arrived in Clewiston at four Friday morning and was fed around ten, with some beans. At Clewiston he was fingerprinted and examined by a doctor and sent to a camp. The food was so bad that many of the cutters bought their food from a commissary, where the scales were weighted against them. Long asked Mr. Mack if he could leave and was told that he couldn't until the season was over. At the end of February Long got a letter from his draft board, calling him up to service. In Alabama he had been told by the man who hired him that he was going to work on a farm belonging to the government and that his would be a national defense job. The colored foremen were always threatening to kill the cutters with their cane knives or to run them into the canals and drown them. If the cutters tried to escape on the highway, the police picked them up and returned them to the plantation. A cutter found on the road without a discharge from the sugar company was jailed for vagrancy. Long worked six weeks, then was discharged.

James Price, who was nineteen, signed up in Memphis at the employment office on Arkansas Street. A white man there told him he would make between a dollar-eighty and three dollars a day. Price assumed he would be working for the government, but this was his own idea based on the name of the company—no one had told him so. He left Memphis the same day on a train with eighty-five other recruits. On arrival they were told they owed nineteen dollars for transportation and a cane knife and a ticket to the mess hall and that money would be deducted from wages to satisfy the debt; a man who stayed the whole season would get the money for his transportation back. They were taken to the fields in the dark and returned in the dark and worked in all weather, regardless of their health.

One night three men slipped away from the Clewiston

camp and ran down the railroad tracks. By the next morning they had walked about eighteen miles. They stopped at a farmhouse for water. Half an hour later they were standing on the highway when a white man drove by them and stopped. He had a sheriff's badge and a gun in a holster. He searched them and found a sugar company badge and took all three to jail. Their supervisor came and got them, put them back in the fields, and told them that if they did that again they would spend nine months in jail. According to one of them, Walter Price, the men started cutting cane as soon as it was light enough to see and worked until dark and they also worked in the rain. Mr. Mack visited the fields about four times a day, carrying a blackjack and a pistol. He cursed the cutters who fell behind and on one occasion Price saw him beat a man for not keeping up. Price fell sick and Mr. Mack would not let him see the doctor until several days had passed. When Price returned to the fields he did not have the strength to keep up. Mr. Mack told him that if he did not work faster he was going to whip him. A week later, Price left the camp at night and never went back. He found work picking beans and stayed at it several months and then went back to Memphis. The records of the company say that he left voluntarily.

Alberta Fisher heard from her son, Earlie, that a white man named Mack had been going up and down Hollywood Street in the black section of Memphis looking for men to cut sugar cane on the plantation of the U.S. Sugar Corporation at Clewiston, Florida. Earlie told her the man was promising free transportation and three dollars a day. Mack took Earlie to the recruitment office on Arkansas Street and another man there gave him a train ticket. A number of young men between seventeen and twenty went with him. One got back to Memphis because his mother hired a lawyer and a woman from the Memphis Juvenile Court helped out. The young man said that the cutters were treated like dogs and beaten, that they began their day at four and worked until sundown, and that mainly they were fed cabbage and beans from a bucket. Mrs. Fisher wrote Earlie and had her letter returned unclaimed. When he made it back to Memphis Earlie told her that he had escaped the plantation by swimming a river with several other boys, one of whom had been shot by a guard. He had been living at the Miami Locks plantation, where Mr. Neal was bossman. When Earlie arrived, he and the others were lined up in front of the plantation store. Mr. Neal told them they didn't owe until they passed the pay window, and that if any of them did not want to work he could walk out the gate. Whoever stayed and took the two dollars Neal was about to advance was in debt. The guard at Earlie's barracks was an old black man who stood by the bridge over the canal and had a stick and a pistol. He was kindly and did not watch them closely and the cutters called him Dad. After several cutters had run off and been brought back to the camp by Mr. Neal, Dad was replaced with a watchman who kept close track of them. Earlie had been at the camp about a week when he and a young man named Red caught a ride on a sugar train headed for Clewiston. A man appeared on the top of the car and shot at them, hitting Red in the arm. Earlie jumped off and returned to the camp. Two weeks later he left at night and never went back.

Robert Mitchell went to Clewiston in November, enticed by the free transportation. He was assigned to the South Shore Plantation and when he arrived the supervisor, O. L. Sheppard, told him and the others with him that they owed fifteen dollars and forty-four cents for transportation, that there would be additional charges for their equipment and identification badges, and that they could not leave until they had retired the debt. The barracks doors were not locked, but Sheppard said that if they tried to run away they'd be shot. After he had been at the camp five days, Mitchell was paid two dollars. For cutting cane he received a dollar-eighty a day. When the first payday arrived, Sheppard told Mitchell he would get no money because he was still in debt to the company. Sheppard always carried a blackjack and a gun. The plantation was guarded by two white men carrying guns. When the cutters walked to and from the sugar cane fields they passed guards at the crossroads. One named J.D. often beat men in the fields. They were roused each morning by a black man who banged on the door of the barracks with a stick. The plantation had no fences around it, only canals. Sheppard told them that the only way to escape was to walk down the highway and that he would catch them if they did. On one occasion Mitchell was in the commissary when Sheppard was present. A cutter asked for an item the store didn't have. The clerk hit the cutter with a milk bottle, and Sheppard kicked him out the door. After Mitchell had been at the camp a month, he and Bubber Sneed and Andrew Gillion waded a canal at three in the morning and ran off through the fields.

William Smith sent money to his son to pay his way home

and got no answer. A month later he sent a telegram asking whether the money had arrived and why there had been no response. He said that if his son could not reply freely he should simply respond "no answer." He got a telegram back, with the message "no answer." Willie Smith was sixteen. He worked three months at Miami Locks, under Mr. Neal. Neal would visit the fields four or five times a day, carrying a pistol and a blackjack, but Smith never saw him use them. He would, however, enter the barracks in the morning and beat cutters who had not got out of bed. This never happened to Smith, but to escape a beating he once ran from the barracks wearing only his pants. After two weeks, Smith fled the camp at night with two other men. They followed the railroad tracks toward Clewiston and by morning reached the Benbow plantation. A white man driving a truck asked them where they were going. One of the three had a sugar company badge and when the white man saw this he put his hand in his pocket as if he had a gun and escorted them to the commissary. That afternoon, Mr. Neal came in his truck and took them back to Miami Locks, saying that if they tried that again they would be hurt.

Virginia Jones in Memphis got a letter from her son Carol, saying he was being held at a prison farm and was not allowed to leave. She got a second letter from him saying he was all right, but she felt it showed he had been forced to write it. Carol and the others were awakened each morning at three by a black man pounding with a stick on the door to the barracks. He would come by again a few minutes later, this time with the supervisor, who would curse at the men still in bed and strike them on their ankles with a blackjack.

When a cutter said he was sick, the supervisor would say, "I brought you down here to work and you'll work, whether you're sick or not." Carol felt that the breakfasts and suppers served by the mess hall weren't too bad, but the noon meal, brought on a truck and served in a bucket, was never very good. One day Neal showed up in the field with a new bull-whip and walked around the field cracking the whip above the heads of the cutters and behind their backs. An older worker told Carol it was pointless to try to escape by hopping one of the sugar trains because the guards aboard them had guns and would use them. Carol wanted to leave but was afraid to. An aunt sent him money to buy a ticket on a bus back to Memphis. He escaped early one morning by walking off down the railroad tracks. Two men wearing caps and badges with the insignia of the company stopped him, but he told them that he was being transferred from one camp to another and they let him go.

Christina Branner wrote her son, Harvey Lee, in Clewiston and had the letter returned marked "not called for." She wrote Mr. Mack, the supervisor, who answered that he had talked to Harvey Lee, who had told him he was staying at the plantation until the end of the season. Harvey Lee was sixteen years old. Some of his friends were planning to run away and asked him to come but he was afraid to. They left without him and were caught and brought back to the fields. Neal said they would be put in jail if they tried again. He said that anyone trying to catch a ride on a sugar train would be shot and that anyone trying to hitch a ride on the highway would be arrested. Harvey Lee worked from three in the morning until after dark. On some nights he would be taken back to the fields and kept there until ten burning cane. He did not believe he got all the money owed him. Before his fourth payday—that is, in his fourth month—Mr. Neal told Harvey Lee and Willie Smith to leave because the FBI had written to him saying he was to let them go. Neal gave him seventy-nine cents, and the two of them left.

Frank Miller signed up in Memphis and was sent to Miami Locks. There he was told that the trip, which had been advertised in Memphis as being free, had cost him fifteen dollars; the money would be deducted from what he earned. Miller told Mr. Neal that the man in Memphis had said that the trip would be free and Neal said he didn't care what the man in Memphis had said, they would all have to stay in Florida until the debt had been paid. Neal told them that anyone who left would not get far before he would catch him and bring him back. Miller arrived in the fields before light and stayed until after dark and a few nights a week returned to burn cane. No one ever mentioned overtime pay. After four weeks, when the first payday arrived, Neal told Miller he would get no money because he was still in debt to the company. The same thing happened the next month. The card he was given to show his earnings had on it a deduction of nine forty-four noted as "miscellaneous," which was mysterious to him. Miller ran away from the camp in the middle of January.

Vernon Lawhorn had gone to the employment office on Arkansas Street, in Memphis, with Dr. Stanley Lutz, a white minister to a black congregation. Lawhorn was assigned to the Bare Branch plantation. Before he went to work Mr. Mack told him and the other new arrivals that no one could leave until the end of the season. Mack told them, "I don't trust any of you black S.O.B.'s, and if any of you want to leave, don't let me catch you." The first week Lawhorn was there the barracks were not locked, but then some cutters ran away, and Mr. Mack had the rest locked in each night at nine. On each occasion when cutters ran away Mr. Mack would gather the rest and say he would kill anyone who left before his debt was retired. Mack carried a gun and so did his two white assistants. While he was at the plantation Lawhorn wrote three letters complaining about conditions. When he got back to Memphis he discovered none had arrived. Mr. Mack told the cutters that when they had letters to mail they should leave them unsealed at the plantation office, along with three cents for the stamp. Lawhorn, Clem Burns, and Roosevelt Amos left the plantation one evening around seven and walked along the railroad tracks until they came to the highway. When they saw the headlights of cars approaching they would hide behind palm trees at the side of the road. By hopping freight trains, they eventually reached Memphis.

Joe Willie Robinson, who was known as Jake and was sixteen, wrote his brother Benjamin two letters describing inhumane conditions at the plantation where he lived. A white man and a white woman at the employment office in Memphis had told Joe Willie that he could make five or six dollars a day in the cane fields. He left Memphis the same day by train and was assigned to the Miami Locks Plantation under Mr. Neal. Neal addressed all the new men in front of the commissary, saying, "I don't know what they told you before you got down here, but you'll have to pay for your transportation, which was fifteen forty-four. That will be deducted from your first month's pay. If you don't want to stay you can go now. I'll give you two dollars for a knife and blanket. If you take it you owe me and you'll have to stay here until you work it out. Don't try to leave. Wherever you go I'll catch you." Neal was always armed with a pistol and a blackjack. Robinson never saw him use the pistol but he saw him use the blackjack once. Robinson said a few boys from Memphis ran away. When Mr. Neal noticed they were gone he collected the rest of them and said he was going to bring back the ones who left. The next day he did. That night he addressed the men in the barracks, saying, "You'd better not run away. I've told the night watchman to watch you closely. It will be too bad for you if you get caught." One night six weeks after he arrived Robinson started hitchhiking on the road toward Clewiston. He had almost reached town when Neal came by in a pickup truck. On the way back to the camp, Neal told him he could never get away, because he would always be caught. Robinson worked three months and never received any money. He was in the habit of drawing five dollars a week. One day he saw Neal knock off the porch of the commissary a man who had asked why the cutters never got any money. Around the first of February Robinson slipped away again, hitchhiking this time in the other direction from Clewiston. He took whatever work he could find in Florida and Georgia and got word from Atlanta to his brother in Memphis, who came down to get him.

Percy Evans, who was twenty-seven and lived with his aunt Belle Hall on Mr. W. E. Bradford's place, in Jackson County, Mississippi, registered in Natchez for work and was taken by truck to Vicksburg, where he joined others being taken to Florida by bus. He stayed two months and escaped with four other men. He was not the object of any violence but saw one man pistol-whipped by a guard.

George Green went to Florida with his brothers Johnnie and Andrew and stayed about thirty days, for which George received no pay above his advances. The black night watchman at the camp told the men that they could not leave and that if they did and were caught they would be beaten and placed in jail. Sheppard, the superintendent, and another white man, Mr. J. D., carried guns. Green saw a cutter who had tried to escape caught and beaten by the white foreman. The cutter was brought back from the highway and beaten by one man while another held a gun on him. When they were finished, they sent the cutter back into the fields.

John Lee Alsobrook was told by Neal when he arrived that he and the other men owed the company for their transportation and could not leave until they had cleared up the debt. Neal said, "If you try to run away before then, I'll catch you and keep you here a lifetime." When Alsobrook joined the line on his first payday, Neal told him to get out of it because he still owed the company and couldn't collect yet for himself. After he had been there three weeks, he and Sam Grey and a few others slipped off and walked all night down the railroad tracks. In the morning a white man in a truck stopped them. One of the cutters carried a blanket from the sugar company. When the white man noticed it he drew a pistol and made them get into his truck. He drove them to the nearest sugar plantation, where he made them sit on the commissary steps while his secretary called Mr. Neal, who arrived a few hours later. On the way back to the plantation,

Neal stopped at a cafe and had two men watch the cutters while he was inside. Back at the camp he took the men to the commissary, where he bought a new blackjack. He stood in front of them striking the blackjack in his hand and said he was going to wear it out on Sam Grey's head. He swung at Grey and missed. He told them, "If you try anything like that again I'll kill you. You'll never get out of here." He took the cutters to the fields and made them work all day for no credit and he replaced the watchman that night. Alsobrook's mother sent him eighteen dollars and when he saw his chance he slipped off and got a bus back to Memphis.

One morning while George Mayfield was sleeping, Mr. Mack came into the barracks and hit him on the head with a blackjack and said it was time to go to work.

On returning to Tuscaloosa or West Memphis, Arkansas or Memphis or Vicksburg, a number of men or their families made complaints to their county solicitors or to the local offices of the FBI, which was already familiar with U.S. Sugar; in 1937 the company had recruited in Georgia and people there complained when they got back from the fields. In February of 1942 the FBI interviewed cutters in Alabama (interviews in Memphis took place in March, July, August, and September, in Mississippi in May and June) and wrote up their statements, which were sent to J. Edgar Hoover, who reminded Assistant Attorney General Wendell Berge (in a memorandum) that the FBI had visited Mr. Von Mach, personnel director for U.S. Sugar, in response to the Georgians' complaints of peonage. Von Mach assured the FBI that no cutters were held against their will or in conditions of peonage. Berge, replying to Hoover, wondered why, if the money owed cutters was paid as Von Mach said it had been, and conditions at the camps were as he described, U.S. Sugar could not find cutters in Florida.

The FBI report is sixty pages and has a preface containing information concerning the background of the company, which includes this interesting entry:

> The United States Sugar Corporation was formed by the Bitting Brothers, Clarence, William and Charles S. Mott, all formerly of General Motors, when the predecessor company formed by Dahlberg Celotex went into receivership.
>
> The Dahlberg Company manufactured a type of wall board from cane sugar by-products. This was unsuccessful and resulted in the loss of about $17,000,000 due principally to the fact that mice ate the product with the sugar content.

A summary says cutters were promised wages between three and six dollars a day and free transportation, as well as housing, board, lights, and water in a company camp. When they arrived they were told they were indebted to the corporation for bus fare and were charged for a blanket, a knife, a cane badge, and board at four-fifty a week. Instead of the figure they were promised, they were paid a dollar-eighty a day. Many cutters complained the plantations were peonage farms they were unable to leave until they had paid off their debts. The superintendents carried blackjacks and guns and said anyone escaping would be charged with vagrancy or hitchhiking and fined and returned to the fields to work off his fine. Cutters at one plantation were permitted to gamble at a game run by Mr. Mack, who took a cut and arrested anyone gambling elsewhere.

The FBI report continues:

> There does not seem to be any dispute over the major facts: that the men are charged for their transportation to Clewiston; that they are not paid the wages promised to them when hired but receive, on the average, about $1.80 per day; that the work day starts before dawn and lasts until dusk, with several nights of 'burning' cane until 10 or 11 o'clock; that the men are allowed to draw small advances two or three days a week and are paid but once a month; that the superintendents, and possibly some of the foremen, are armed with pistols and blackjacks; that the food furnished to the men is not of the best and that they are charged five cents a gallon for fresh water; that it is customary for the superintendent of the plantation to come into the barracks after the nightwatchman has awakened the men by banging on the door with a stick and use a blackjack to awaken the men who are still in bed. However, there is a dispute as to whether or not the men are locked in the barracks at night; whether the camps are guarded by armed men and whether the men are free to leave the employ of the company. There does not seem to be any dispute as to the fact that those men who have attempted to escape from the plantations and

> are picked up on the highway or shot at while trying to hitch rides on the sugar trains are returned to the plantations and forced to work.

The report then says that a woman at the state employment service in Tuscaloosa gave a statement in which she said that she referred Negro workers to the sugar cane employers and that she had heard talk of complaints but thought that either the Negroes were afraid to complain to her or that they had nothing to complain about except the hard work.

Cutters named Millard Jones, James Maddox, Joe Steward, and Franklin Mosley made statements to the FBI agents in favor of the company. They say they have never heard of anyone's being prevented from leaving, that none of the foremen is armed, that the watchmen are there to prevent fights and watch for fires, that some men run off but they are ones in debt, that they themselves are satisfied with their jobs, and that most of the complaints come from city Negroes who are accustomed to city life and unfit to work all day in the fields.

Von Mach, the personnel manager, told the FBI that the workers are promised free transportation only if they complete the harvest, in order to prevent the men from traveling to Florida at the expense of the company, then leaving to work for someone else. He said that cutters are paid a dollar-eighty to start but that at the end of two weeks they may choose to work at a piece rate paid by the ton or to continue at the daily rate. Paid by the ton, a good worker could make as much as four dollars a day. He said that a cutter is paid what he is owed upon being discharged, although a discharge is not easy to get. The company made it difficult because many workers would ask for a discharge, then return several days later, which meant giving them another physical, plus a new badge. He said that all supervisors had been instructed not to abuse employees or to interfere in any way with their liberty, nor are any superintendents allowed to carry guns or blackjacks or intimidate employees.

Mr. Mack, whose full name was Evan Ward McLeod, told the agents that he never mistreated or threatened anyone and denied that he ever carried a blackjack or a gun. He said that he had never had an employee arrested for vagrancy and that no employee had ever been forced to work off a fine on the plantation. He also denied that there was a bar on the plantation where gambling took place or that he took a cut from the proceeds of any gambling.

McLeod's statement, on page fifty-eight, is followed on fifty-nine by George Mayfield's saying that two months earlier McLeod had hit him on the head with a blackjack and told him it was time to go to work.

The report concludes with an index having entries under five headings: references in investigative reports to instances of threats (thirteen); . . . to instances of the return of escaped victims to conditions of peonage (ten); . . . to shooting of escaping peons or arrests for vagrancy (four); . . . to gambling game and that McLeod was deputy sheriff (two) . . . to instances of beatings (twelve).

Assistant Attorney General Berge had a copy of his memo to Hoover sent to the U.S. Attorney in Tampa, who gave the FBI report to a grand jury (in Hillsborough County), which delivered an indictment against U.S. Sugar, as well as against

M. E. Von Mach, Evan Ward McLeod, Oliver H. Sheppard, and ——— Neal. (At the time of the indictment it had not been known that Mr. Neal's name was Neal Williamson.) In addition to one count of peonage, they were charged with one count of conspiracy to violate "the right and privilege . . . of citizens to be free from slavery . . . and the right and privilege of . . . citizens to the free exercise and enjoyment of freedom from slavery and involuntary servitude secured to . . . citizens by the Thirteenth Amendment of the Constitution of the United States. . . ."

The four were arrested in November 1942. Each made his bail of one thousand dollars. Lawyers for each filed motions ("Said count fails to allege . . ."; "Said count is duplicitous . . ."; "Said count wholly and totally fails . . ."; "Said count is fatally defective . . ."). Meanwhile U.S. Sugar argued that it could not as a corporation be held accountable to laws made for individuals. In April the indictment was quashed. The U.S. Attorney did not attempt to have it revived.

What happened is the lawyers had discovered a flaw in the way the grand jury had been selected. During the August before the indictment, a district judge had ordered that names be added to the jury box so that the list of people available to serve included at least three hundred. The clerk added one thousand one hundred and fifty names, all from Hillsborough County, although the grand jury represented fourteen counties. This was done to avoid difficulties of travel during the period of wartime gas shortages; all twenty-three men selected to sit on the jury lived in Tampa. The lawyers argued that people who live in Hillsborough County, of which Tampa is part, were prejudiced against U.S. Sugar and its employees. Proof of this, they said, was that two years earlier Hillsborough papers had carried a report of a speech by Florida Senator Claude Pepper to the Tampa Chamber of Commerce in which Pepper said that he did not think he would be able to convince Congress to increase sugar acreage allocations until the share belonging to U.S. Sugar (eighty-six per cent) was reduced. Senator Pepper said Congress saw no reason to encourage a corporate monopoly, and that he hoped to see smaller growers participating in the increase of acreage.

Among the members of the grand jury were a teacher, a clerk at an oil company, a salesman of dry goods, an architect, a bridge contractor, a president of an interior design firm, two tailors, a butler, a man in advertising, a coffee broker, and the treasurer of a produce company. No farmers. Therefore, said the lawyers, the jury was "without knowledge of the intricate problems as between agriculture and labor."

The judge overlooked the reference to Claude Pepper's speech but ruled that the grand jury was illegally drawn and "Ordered and Adjudged that for reasons herein stated the said indictment in this cause be and the same is hereby quashed and declared to be null and void."

By the time the judge signed his order, in April 1943, arrangements had already been made to bring to America the West Indians who would work in the cane fields the following season.

22

Growers of vegetables in south Florida had for some time been including men from the Bahamas in their harvest crews. In the December of 1942, one of the growers, on behalf of them all and with the endorsement of Florida Congressman Cannon, sent the Department of Agriculture a contract he said growers would sign to bring as many men as possible from the Bahamas to fill spots on harvest crews where sufficient American labor could not be found. The grower wrote that the farmers all favored the use of the Bahamians because, as well as being capable and eager for the jobs, the Bahamians would be easy to bring to the country, their islands being so close. In addition, he wrote, "The vast difference between the Bahama Island labor and domestic, including Puerto Rican is that the labor transported from the Bahama Islands can be deported and sent home, if it does not work, which cannot be done in the instance of labor from domestic United States or Puerto Rico."

Because the Bahamas were not large enough to supply all the men needed, the government turned to Jamaica, the largest island in the Caribbean where English was spoken. On May 11, 1943—that is, in the spring before the Jamaicans arrived in Florida—George Hill, working for the Deputy Administrator of the War Food Administration, the agency superintending the importation of the workers, wrote the Acting Chief of the Division of Farm Population and Rural Welfare, a part of the Bureau of Agricultural Economics:

> As you are aware, we are placing Jamaican workers in certain areas of our country to help make up the deficit among agricultural laborers.
>
> These people, while mostly belonging to the negro race, have a set of mores and social patterns radically different from those of the American negro. I am told that there is little race distinction on the island. Because of this difference it may not be advisable for us to encourage the placement of these workers in the areas of our country which customarily employ American negro labor.
>
> Has your division made any studies that might help us in this matter or do you know personally of literature in this field? Do you know of any experiences in the past where Jamaicans have been used in our southern states? I will appreciate whatever information you can secure for me.

A week later Hill wrote the Deputy Administrator of the War Food Administration:

> I have been checking around on the question of using Jamaican workers in the South and get the following picture.
>
> Over a period of years some Jamaicans have been working in coastal communities from Miami to Norfolk. However, experience with these workers has been that States' Negroes are more amenable to acceptance of the traditional local racial differentials. Summing up all of the evidence, I cannot get anyone very enthusiastic over the idea of placing Jamaicans where employers are accustomed to using States' Negroes.
>
> When peak season develops, however, and there is really a critical need for labor, Jamaicans will probably be accepted. To start out, we should attempt to place them where States' Negroes have not been used.

The government of Jamaica insisted that its citizens be assigned only to farms north of the Mason–Dixon line. The Jamaicans were brought over on ships landed in Florida. The first to arrive was the S.S. *Shanks*, which had bunks for seventeen or eighteen hundred men and brought four thousand. During the trip the *Shanks* ran out of water. A man was lost overboard. The Jamaicans had been told to bring shaving kits, but when they got to America their razors and bay rum were confiscated by Military Police. The MP's also took any rum they found among the Jamaicans' belongings. The Jamaicans worked through the spring and the summer on farms in the northeast. Those who came to the cane fields in the fall signed contracts accepting the work and extending their stays. When they got to the fields many of them changed their minds. They worked poorly or not at all and said that they had had no idea what they were getting into when they signed on. A number were sent home. Those who stayed began to make a little money and apparently were satisfied with the arrangement.

The next year, 1944, Jamaicans were recruited specifically to work in the sugar cane harvest. During the season beginning in the fall of 1945, many Jamaicans complained about conditions at the U.S. Sugar plantations. Fearing that antagonisms between cutters and supervisors might turn violent, the Jamaican government called its men home. They were replaced by men from Barbados. The following year, U.S. Sugar promised to improve conditions at the camps and the Jamaicans returned.

23

With C. and A.: We had just driven out to Shawnee Farm a few days after our first visit and had found no one to talk to and had driven back to town.

Anthony said, "Where you all want to go now, man?"

Caveman said, "Hey, go round to Miss Blunting," and Anthony said, "Hey, you think it's summer?" Anthony saw some girls by the side of the road. He was driving my rented car. He waved to the girls and they waved back. "Now at night they say, 'Anthony, where you keep your car at?' 'I let my brother keep it.' 'I just saw your brother.' 'I mean my *older* brother.' "

We drove into a yard in Harlem. There was a man standing beside a house. Anthony said, "Weren't you at the Chinese Farm a minute ago?"

The man studied us. He was older. He said no.

Anthony said, "You go out to the Chinese Farm, you see a man just like you."

Caveman said to Anthony, "Where that tall dude live that married Felix? He used to cut cane, didn't he?"

"He never really cut it, he just picked it up."

Anthony pulled out of the driveway. He rolled down his window. The man was still watching us. Anthony said, "I believe you in two damn places at one time!"

We drove to the end of the block. A man with a cowboy hat walked toward us. Anthony said, "Ain't you a Jamaican?"

The man said, "Hell yeah, and I'm a Barbadian, too. Look out for me!" He walked into the yard where the other man was standing. I looked back as we pulled away and he was giving us an enormous wave.

Anthony said, "Man, he look *lit*."

We drove through the center of Harlem.

Anthony said, "Where you want to go?"

Caveman said, "Look for some more of those Jamaicans."

We passed a woman dancing on the porch of a house. Anthony shouted out, "Hey, I come by your house tonight." The woman, in a theatrical way, put her hands on her cheeks and made her eyes large and yelled, "No!" and then broke out laughing.

We drove into Clewiston. Anthony said, "Damn, I was going to surprise my lady tonight."

Caveman said, "What were you going to do? Give her a rose?"

"Hell, no. I was going to go home, clean up some, kiss her, then tell her about the tire."

A young woman walking along the street by the mill saw

Anthony at the wheel and yelled out, "Hey, Anthony, who car?"

Anthony yelled back, "Mine."

She said, "How much down?"

Anthony said, "A thousand," and waved.

24

Driving by Benbow one afternoon I picked up a Jamaican on his way from the Moore Haven camp to the commissary at Benbow. He was older than most of the cutters I had seen. He told me he was fifty and in his fourteenth season. I said, "You must cut pretty fast," and he said, "Yeah." I said, "You must have made a lot of money today," and he said, "The price not so pretty today."

25

The cutters who live out in the country at home do better with the contract than the ones who live in the city. Cutters living in the country are able to buy land and build houses, usually of poured cement. They can feed themselves from what they grow. They can harvest wild fruit. Those living in the cities and in the larger towns or around the resorts cannot possibly afford to buy homes. All of them rent, and none at attractive prices.

Although the cutters who live in the country live with land all around them, their own holdings, if they have any, are likely to be less than one acre and not likely to exceed two and a half acres. Two professors at the University of South Florida, Terry McCoy and Charles Wood, have specialized in the circumstances of the cane cutters at home. They say that they have noticed that cane cutting in America never seems to buy the cutter a ticket out of his circumstances. At best the cutters end up marginally improving their lot. When they retire from the work, they become dependent on others.

The white people in the industry like to say that the opportunity to cut sugar cane in south Florida changes the lives of the men who accept it. The white people like to say that the money those men make in America is used at home to buy a house, or land, or cattle, or a gasoline-powered generator. They like to talk about the cutter who over the years worked steadily and with enough application that he made the money for his son to be trained as a dentist, but they can never recall his name, or what island he was from, or what grower he worked for, or exactly what years he spent on the contract.

It was once put forth by the sugar cane industry that cutters helped the economy of their islands by hiring people to look after their farms or to tend their goats while they were in Florida, but that was discovered not to be true. When the cutters go on the contract the responsibility of keeping up their interests, whatever ones they might have, falls to the women and to their children.

The white people in Florida say that although work cutting sugar cane is available in the islands, especially in Jamaica, the men who cut in America scorn this work at home. Many white people say that a Jamaican considers as his inferior a man who cuts sugar cane at home. The cutters say they do not cut sugar cane at home because the pay without the exchange rate is not as good as it is in America, because the season for harvest in Jamaica begins a few weeks after they return from the contract and they would be too tired to take part anyway, and because the hard soil there makes the work more difficult; the knife dulls faster in striking the soil and the soil does not give as the muck does. In any case the crop is not large enough on any of the islands to provide work for even as many as a small portion of those who go to America, nor would it be of any help to the men from the cities.

It is clear that the cutters would never cut cane if work were available for them at home.

26

The most persistent menace to sugar cane in Florida is frost. Cold air arrives mainly from the northwest. Crossing the Lake, it may rise in temperature several degrees. Growers classify land as warm or cold. Warm land is less likely to suffer frost; most of it is land that is closer to the Lake. Bottom land and land farthest from the lake freeze first, which means that most of the sand land is cold land. After three or four days frozen cane dries up and turns brown. One can then trace the progress of the cold by the pattern in the fields. Freezes are extremely specific. A field may be damaged on one side of a road and not on the other. Or a row stand intact beside ones that have withered. The pattern is not haphazard; it mainly reflects characteristics of the land, not eccentricities of the weather. After a freeze growers tour their fields, then revise their harvest to send first to the mill what is damaged.

The most likely moment for a punishing freeze is the full moon of February. Growers whose fields reach the waning moon breathe easier. Serious freezes seem to occur in cycles of nine years. Occasionally a freeze is total—that is, includes the whole crop. Each time a field endures a frost, it returns fewer tons. Unless the freeze is particularly severe, the cane does not perish. At twenty-two degrees the stalk cracks, and the cracks provide an entry for bacteria, which eventually kill the plant. A freeze of any consequence kills the terminal bud, which starts shoots called la-las growing from the stalk at the joints. La-las are full of water, which dilutes the sucrose during milling; a second freeze, if there is one, kills them. The rest of the stalk can be milled as many as three months later. As a rule, however, a grower has thirty to forty days following a freeze to get all his cane at a profit. Growers expect to lose ten per cent of their crop to frost. Hand-cutting becomes particularly efficient after a freeze. The supervisors examine the cane and tell the leadmen where to have the cutters chop the stalk so they send only clean cane to the mill. The top of the stalk is more vulnerable to frost than the bottom; the ground warms the air. In addition, concentrations of sucrose in the base of the stalk are more resistant to the cold. People say that sucrose is the antifreeze in sugar cane.

27

Caveman wanted one night to go to Belle Glade, so we drove down and went to three bars. Then we stood on the sidewalk and watched the line of cars waiting to use the drive-up window at Everglades Liquors. A man asked a woman standing next to me for her phone number and she said, "Eight, seven, three, something, something, never-mind, never-mind." Then a young man left the doorway of a club across the street. Caveman called to him and he came over and Caveman introduced him as Star Child. Star Child told me he was trying to scratch out a living as a disc jockey in the local clubs. Caveman told him that I was trying to meet some Jamaicans. Star Child said he could help with that. He took us across the street and back into the bar we had come from. He disappeared among the crowd. Caveman and I stood there about three minutes. I bought Caveman a pint of wine. The volume of the music made it awkward to talk. Over the shoulders of a couple of men I saw Star Child speaking with a man who looked Jamaican. I saw the man shake his head. Then I saw Star Child go out a door by the side of the bar. He came back a moment later and motioned to us to follow him. Outside were several West Indians leaning against a car parked at the curb. When they saw me they separated and each walked off in a different direction. Star Child said, "What you doing that for?" He tried to get them back but couldn't and came over to me and said, "They think you are there to get them in trouble, jeopardize their working in cane."

We went to the 2001 Club down the block, following Star Child, but when we walked in Caveman turned us around abruptly and walked us out. All I saw was a stage and some beaded curtains. Caveman saw either someone he didn't want to see, or someone he thought might not want to see me. We went out and stood on the street corner. A woman came up to Caveman and said, "What you want?" and Caveman said, "Well, if you giving it away." She said, "I ain't giving nothing away." Then Caveman left for a few minutes. I stood on the corner, next to a pregnant woman. A man walked by and looked at her stomach. She said, "Why you looking at me? Some these women be getting eight and nine kids and you looking at me like I can't even get one." Then Caveman came back and we decided to leave. On the way back to Clewiston we saw Star Child hitchhiking and picked him up. Star Child said he was sorry he had not been able to arrange anything for me. Caveman said, "Those dudes keep their stuff in*doors*." He asked Star Child if he had ever cut cane. Star Child said, "I don't see it's worth the russle and tussle." We left Star Child off in Harlem and then I took Caveman home. We agreed to meet the next evening. "You tell me when you want me," he said. "We going to find some Jew*mai*cans tomorrow."

28

A. St. Lucian:

"My father used to come to America some regular cutting cane. He traveled here about twenty-five seasons, then he retired, and decided to give his sons a try—we are four brothers, and I am the second—which they never wanted to take it on, so they pass it to me. My father tell us that the work is full of a hard something like, and when he tell the other brothers they shake their heads and decide to stay home. So I put myself on a mission to my father. He ask me to work hard and he ask me to get along good with the people. There were twelve of us from St. Lucia in the camp; some got sent home: one cut his thumb off, another used to get sick regular, another run away, and another they sent to Atlantic Sugar Company on a transfer.

"One thing I find: using the cutlass is a skillful trade. It is a dangerous weapon, and if you not skillful you getting hurt all the time. Sometimes just when you board the bus and hold it wrong, it cuts you. I sharpen it every single day. You have to be passing the file on it some regular. If it be dull, you feel the cane heavy like, and it break down your physical. Every time I reach the camp I wash the bill and let it dry and then I sharpen it. When I starting, some men actually hold my knife and say 'Francis, this is the way to cut the cane; now conduct yourself in this manner.' Many, many times I cut myself. When you don't know how to use the bill, you always getting touch and touch and touch. I think I have cut all my five fingers already. I got my boot chopped up to the fullest; I feel if I don't have these boots my feet be cut up right now. Anytime I get cut, I cure very fast. Whether I feel the pain or not, I wrap the damage and still go to work.

"Cutting the cane in itself is also a skillful task, you must be skillful at it. When you cutting the cane you must have a free mind. You must not be frightened. You must try not to go in a doubt. To the point where you go in a doubt, you will never make your money for that day. In other words, take an example, you go in and you want to go, or you don't want to go in that field that morning, you must go in *sure*. I come here to work and rather than putting any other thing in my mind I put cane cutting in my mind. You have to say I'm going through that row and go *through* it. You don't know who is who, which is which, what is what.

"In the training time bossman always used to tell me, must first cut the stubble low, must pile the cane good, throw the trash away good, then develop some speed, so that you do not get check out for slow, and anytime that you get check out for slow in those days after the eight days' training, they will be sending you back to your country, but getting check out for any other thing—too many stubble, for bad piling, or high stubble—that just get you finish for the day. I got checked out once only, for high tops, carelessness. The reason why I got checked out, I saw a nice piece of cane field and decided to go through it like mad, which is the first time I was ever choosing so much work for the day. In working the cane there is much things that you must observe, you must be exact at every single thing, you must be watching, you must have so many things on your mind; cane-wise you must be saying that you do not want to get checked out, you must make sure you cut the tops right, that you pile right, and that you develop enough speed so that you make your day's work. I was only concentrating on the point of piling the cane and the low stubble, but not on the tops; I was just cutting like mad. When I reach a quarter row, the bossman pass me and he say, 'Too many tops from the beginning.' He have to give me a check-out, that would learn me a lesson so that the next time I cut cane I have to concentrate on every single thing. Many times if I do something wrong the bossman come and tell me, 'Francis, your tops is too high,' or I have too high stubble, and sometime he cut it, but sometimes if he be mad at it he call you back, and if he call me back I feel like it is a fight down, but still I can manage to do a day's work. I look more into the spiritual side in this world than I do the physical side. The spiritual will bring help to me when I am tired or when Babylon set-ups have me down-pressed. Anytime I been fight down I call on the Lord strongly. I call his help, and I get help most of the time.

"I work harder in the evening. The heat is then in my body and the work is in me. I develop more speed and all the muscles in me have been stretched out. I feel the morning cold hard; it get my fingers numb, and to the point that it burn me I can't go through the cane the way I want to go through it. Your whole body, your fingers and everything, numb. Most time I go in the field, while the sun rising I praise the morning sun so that I get strength right through the day.

"When I wake up I take care of myself by washing, and after then right away they will take us out of the barracks for breakfast. I try to eat a heavy breakfast because sometimes when my belly hit me I get set back in the field. If you leave your row to eat, gone to another man. After breakfast we put on two pants for the field. On the bus everybody will try to sit by the door. Sometimes when we reach the field it is still dark and we can hardly see; every man will hustle to get a good row. I get cut many times when we rush out the door, and I cut one man then too. Sometimes you standing on a row and a man come up and tell you 'This is my partner,' and then you just have to go because you can't fight him. I never let myself get accustomed to anything in this world so that if I lose it, I miss it."

A while later: "I have not worked for some time, maybe ten days, maybe two weeks. I cut myself. I was sharpening the cutlass. I took it and was shaping the handle—it was a new cutlass—making the handle feel good in my palm and just like that on the hand there was blood. The same day I go to work; I tape the hand. Too much pain and it not heal, just open the wound. But to the point I get cut, I knew I would get cut. My dreams tell me that. So I know."

29

Sometimes the cutters call the knife a collins and sometimes they call it the bill. Cutting the cane low they call billing it, or they say they have to bill down the cane. They call it a bill because it makes them their money. When they arrive at the airport in Miami, the liaison officers, the men whose job it is to mediate disputes between the cutters and the growers, ask them if they know where they are going, and when they say no, the liaison officer says, "You are going to drive a collins," and when he says do you know what that is, and they say no, sir, he says, "A collins is a cane knife."

30

Driving a back road one night through fields outside Moore Haven I saw a long low building, like a dance hall, with several houses built from cement block beside it and a couple of trailers and a parking lot where one light shone on a couple of cars. I asked someone a few days later about it and was told it was a roadhouse where cutters went for sport. When I mentioned it to Caveman, he said we could go there.

Anthony drove us and when we arrived two white men and two black were standing in the parking lot warming themselves at a fire in an oil drum. Anthony pulled up slowly beside them. Most of the lights in the cabins were out and the bar was dark. It was nine. One of the men said that the bar had just closed. Caveman asked when it would be open and one of them said that the old man who owned it opened and closed it whenever he felt like it. They told us to come back another time. We drove to Moore Haven. In the back part of town we saw a young woman at the window of a house trailer. She was standing just inside the curtain and she waved. Anthony said, "Damn," and backed up the car. The woman appeared in the frame of the open door. Anthony said, "Hey, baby, come out and ride with us." She said, "I don't ride with strangers." Anthony said, "We won't be strangers after we ride a while." She didn't move. She was standing with her feet on the door sill and leaning forward with one hand on the door jamb and the other against the handle of the screen door. Anthony called out a man's name and asked if she knew where he lived. She said that she was from Jacksonville and didn't know anyone local. Anthony said, "Well, I'm from Jacksonville." He said, "I got a guy here in the back says he knows you. Said he's been knowing you all his life." She said, "What's his name?" Anthony said, "His name is *Cave*man!" "Well, all right," she said, "I'll be seeing you," and stepped back inside and closed the door. As we moved off I saw the curtain part and a man look out at us.

We drove back to Harlem. There had been a rain and you could smell the scent of the fields mixed with the rain, then the smell of ash, then the smell of the pasture, so that even with your eyes closed, or in the darkness, you could tell the shape of the country.

31

A thing to do with a gold tone watch that has a brushed metal face, a sweep hand, a date display, a metal band, and perhaps a piece of red cut glass set in the face like a ruby is sell it at a sugar cane camp. Cutters love watches. Peddlers stick their fingers through the flexible metal wrist bands of several at a time and stroll through the barracks. The cutters ask how many jewels. The peddlers reply, "Seventeen." The cutters never wear their watches into the field for fear the watches will get dirty and break, and they never go into town without them.

Some camps tolerate peddlers, some regard them as trespassers. Camps with commissaries call the sheriff. Where they are unwelcome, they wait until dark to visit. Or park across the road, out of sight of the superintendent's office, or nearby, on land they believe not to be sugar company land, and send a boy in to let the cutters know where the peddler is waiting and what he has brought. Mainly they visit on paydays, but occasionally in between. Different camps often have different pay schedules; if a peddler has driven far into the country to hit one camp, he will drop by any others in the area to see what he can stir up. Some camps share paydays; on those days the peddlers race from one camp to another in a state of anxiety. They are intensely competitive; sometimes when one feels another is prospering, he will report him to the sheriff.

Where the companies allow them, the peddlers set up outside the farm office in the afternoon, shortly before the money is paid out, in order to catch the cutters with cash in their hands. They park their vans alongside the path the cutters take to the barracks and open the doors and place on the grass or a card table some blenders or drink glasses with pictures of the President on them or sneakers or the kind of men's dress shoes made from imitation leather that are sold from racks in big rural department stores. Maybe acrylic rugs with the portrait of a tiger. Perhaps toasters, radios, tape players, fans, practically any kind of appliance. Peddlers selling vegetables rig scales with hanging baskets from the back of their vans. Others hang dresses and pants and shirts from their trunk lids or open the car doors and hang them from the frame, or from the roofs and doors of their vans. Some bring display racks.

Some peddlers, usually men raised in the Caribbean who live now in Miami or West Palm Beach, specialize in supplying products popular at home: S.S.S. Tonic (for rich red blood); Dr. King's Sulphur Bitters (a purge); Eucalyptus Oil (for coughs); Ferrol Tonic (colds); carbolic soap; Dr. Watts

Kidney and Bladder Pills (a diagram on the box shows a body with *x*'s drawn on its back and says, "Your pain is here when your kidneys need help."); castor oil; Dr. Morse's Indian Root Pills (another purge); and tiger balm. A cook at one camp sells perfume and copies videotapes. Jamaicans are fond of hats; they call them felts. They like porkpies that they buy a little small and that ride high on their heads. Another popular item is underwear for their wives and girlfriends. The cutters prefer it in violet, turquoise, black, or red, with as much lace as possible. Some women cook fried chicken and slabs of fish with spices and walk through the barracks selling from the skillet. Peddlers selling gold chains tell the cutters how happy their wives or girlfriends will be to receive them. Cutters weigh the chains in their hands. Sometimes they pull a hair from their heads, hold it to the chain, then release it and note whether it falls or adheres. If it falls they refuse to buy, or try to bargain down the price. They believe that their hair will stick to pure gold.

Many of the peddlers are Arabs from Belle Glade, where they have stores on Avenue A, a main street. Several blocks of Avenue A consist almost entirely of stores owned by Arabs serving the cutters. The stores mainly occupy low, deep, flat-roofed, glass-fronted buildings. Nearly all have awnings. Approximately half have conventional names such as Jay's Fashions and Belle Glade Clothing Store, and half have exotic names such as Shatara Brothers, Yasmin's Fashions, and Hayyeh Department Store. The name of one store is a concession to its clientele (Hi-Style), and one is enigmatic (Nicaragua Store). In the window of Glades Mercantile Furniture is a small sign that says "Nou Pale Creole," an enticement to the Haitians. None of the stores has fixed hours; they stay open as late as there are cutters on the street. Peddlers often advance credit, but the stores will not; they have layaway plans. Many are owned by members of the same family. In at least one of the stores, if you ask how did it occur that a group of Arabs came to reside in an obscure American town with a damp climate and a landscape unlike any found in their country, the proprietor may say that he and his compatriots are American citizens and have the right to live anywhere the hell they want. As it happens, the Arabs live in all parts of Belle Glade. That their stores are grouped together they say is coincidence; Avenue A, being near the camp, is the best location for business. Arabs are not given to settling together, they say. They say you find Arabs in Beverly Hills and you find them in Watts.

Cutters are scornful of merchants and peddlers. They call them Joe Grind, which is a name with three meanings. Joe Grind is the man who romances the wives and girlfriends while the cutters are away. "A man take over at your home, that is Joe Grind," says a cutter. "Joe Grind also the store man, who just want your money. Joe Grind the peddler's a different Joe Grind, because I don't believe that's legal to hustle, to sell without a store." Some of the stores hire cutters from the camp in Belle Glade to stand in their doorways in the evening and lure prospects. When a cutter walks in the proprietor says, "Hey, Joe," and the cutter says, "Yeah, Joe," as if it made him tired to say it.

No item in any of the stores bears a price tag. A cutter asks; the proprietor rarely names a price more than once. The Arabs say that to the cutter a ticket price is irrelevant.

He disregards it. What price the Arab quotes depends on how close he is to the end of the season and how long the object has been part of his stock. He says that the cutter always wants an item for a price roughly equal to what the storekeeper paid for it. A man too eager to sell, who responds too quickly with a price or is too accommodating, makes the cutters nervous; they usually leave.

The Arabs are mainly from Palestine, Jordan, and Israel, particularly the West Bank. They sit on lawn chairs behind their counters; sometimes when you walk in you see only the tops of their heads. The doors stand open for ventilation. What light there is is shadowy and comes through the windows from the street; to illuminate the interior would only enforce the impression of heat. When you walk in from the brighter light the objects inside the store come slowly into focus while your eyes adjust to the light. Fans turn on the counters. Solemn, dark-haired children work the dials on radios or stare out the windows at the traffic. Behind the counter their fathers, or uncles, drink strong sweet Arabian coffee from thermoses. They say it wakes you up, especially after a meal. Unless it suits them, they don't stir until they feel certain of a customer. If they decide a cutter has been standing around, say, a television, or a set of dishes honoring the Bicentennial long enough to make him a prospect, they call out a price from their chair.

The Arabs stock their inventory from trade shows and wholesalers and occasionally at auctions of unclaimed merchandise. They visit trade shows in Miami, New York, Dallas, and Las Vegas. In Dallas they buy western clothes and appliances. In Las Vegas they buy calculators and radios and tape players and pen knives and ashtrays that say "I ♥ Las Vegas." At the end of the harvest they sometimes travel to New Jersey and sell there, or follow the trail of migrant workers through the Midwest. Some return to Jerusalem, where they have houses.

The cutters ship what they have bought in plastic barrels supplied by the Arabs. Some barrels originally held pimiento paste, some held paper products, and some held photographic chemicals. The Arabs charge ten dollars for the barrel, although if a cutter has bought regularly from a merchant or has made a large purchase he will often throw the barrel in free. The Arabs buy the barrels from a supplier in Miami who rounds them up from the warehouses where they originally arrived. Sometimes near the end of the season the Arabs post a boy with a power drill on the sidewalk beside a display of barrels. The boy drills a hole through the top and the lip of the barrel, and the cutter fits a lock through the hole.

Each year the cutters take home quantities of soaps, for themselves and as gifts, as well as toothpaste, toilet paper, and paper towels, all of which are expensive at home. Ones who live without power in the country take batteries for their tape players and radios. Whatever the cutters send home, they feel they pay for three times: to buy, to ship, and to claim at Customs. When the barrels arrive is unpredictable. Sometimes not for months. They are shipped in lots. Periodically the men get on a bus and go down to the harbor in Kingston and stand around at the entrance to the warehouse and check on their arrival, which means killing time at the gate until the man in charge shows up carrying a clipboard and can answer a question.

On paydays the Arabs load their vans so that they resemble condensed versions of their stores. If they have a son they take him with them on their route; the boys sometimes complain that their fathers make them go out and sell even though they don't want to. The Arabs leave their wives or mothers in charge of the store. The women wear scarves on their heads that fall down their backs while they sit in the lawn chairs. The men race to the camps, passing each other on the narrow, curving back roads.

In addition to visiting the Arabs' stores the cutters in Belle Glade shop and eat and drink and party in a number of other places within walking distance of the camp. There is the Rose Beer Garden (next to Linell's House of Beauty); there is the Hollywood Restaurant (painted on the wall outside: "Just Be Good Inside" and "Have Some Fun"); there is Kosmotique (discount beauty and barber supplies); the BM Grocery Poor Folks Store; the 2001 Disco Bar; the Tip Top Restaurant; Positive Vibrations (a record store); the Blue Bell Bar Lounge Super Disco; the E & V Bar; and the Uncle Sam People Place, for beer and wine.

In the late nineteen-seventies the State Department brought men and women preparing for careers in the foreign service to Belle Glade, because the Department believed it was a place where the trainees could experience the poverty, stress, and decay of a third-world country. During their time in Belle Glade they lived in the Holiday Inn, now out of business.

32

Most of the cutters are recruited for the growers by the Florida Fruit and Vegetable Association. U.S. Sugar recruits its own. Representatives interview the candidates at their islands. They are said to reject men whose palms are smooth and uncallused on the assumption that they are unaccustomed to physical work, to reject masons for being too muscular, and fishermen for being prone to trouble with their backs. Any candidate with dreadlocks cuts his hair for his interview, since the recruiters are known not to favor Rastafarians.

The cutters' welfare is seen to by liaison officers, who work for the West Indies Central Labor Organization. The cutters feel the liaison officers are compromised by concern over losing their jobs if they antagonize the growers. They have no faith in the officers' powers. They rarely consult them.

33

An older man:

"I worked fifteen years cane cutting. I came here from Barbados, October twenty-second, in 1958; that was at Runyon Camp, in Belle Glade. At that time it was pretty tough. It was what I call partially slaving yourself. It was what I call a kind of a way a man had to do all that he could in his body to make a dollar.

"The companies put ads in the papers: who would like to go to America and cut cane? Then they came to the labor organization centers and interviewed you proper. I mean real explanatory. A man ask if you eat rice and pork, he ask if you eat hog knuckles and rice, he ask if you eat pinto beans. He show you a cane knife. He tell you that where you work it would be like hell. He tell you there is a stipulation out there: if you don't cut your row like you supposed to, the foreman checks you out; your day is through. The hard talk wasn't nothing to downspirit you; it was something to give you courage. He wanted to make sure you have the equipment to withstand the everyday plunging, trudging, and boring task.

"Next he select this one and that one. You go to the blood people, check your blood, you go to the venereal people, check your venereal, then you hit that plane.

"Where you live it was something like a military depot, but it was just a cane cutting depot. But it had the same stipulations, when you could come and go. Wire and fences.

"After work we would sit around, talk, watch TV. Sometimes if you go in and you too tired to watch TV, you lay upon your bed. You close your eyes to rest and the next day started already when your eyes open.

"When I leave and go home the most thing I did was go fishing. They won't give you a job, because you have been to America and now they think you are set. I'll tell you something: I have one brother living and my mother had eleven children—ten boys and one girl. Only living are me and my older brother. They all died. That was in the days of polio and epilepsy. Then was the days of nonunderstanding of the kinds of medicines and drugs. Whooping cough, epilepsy, and all those things used to take children away from this world. So I saved my money and I could live off it economically, and an economical system is stability. Live with what you can live with and don't live with what you wants to get. Everybody needs a little more, but if the more ain't coming, why try to kill yourself? Make it on what you got. In this cane cutting I have bought three homes in my country. It means I had the ability to work and the mind to continue by the help of the company and the Great Supreme.

"Cane cutting is not something you already learned; you just come up here and they say jump to it. You may cut cane for a week or so and figure your body can't take it, and you say you want to go home, and they will send you home, or they will coax you and coax you, because they need your body in the field. In Barbados you paid by the ton; a man don't have to cut a mile of cane to get a pocket of money. When we came to America, we thought we would be paid by the ton, but when we got here and was addressed as to what we would be doing, we was told that your money starts at the beginning of the row. Then it was up to you to work it out with the brain or whatever common judgment you got; they don't bring you here to have no party.

"You have to cut deep because where the stubbles is is where the sugar is. It's supposed to be cut right down to the dirt; they don't want that sugar in the ground, they want that in the truck, they want that cane in the sugar mill to grind.

"You change partners to find someone whose speed is compatible. All season changing. They got some fellows that is smart on the game, and it is still a game in the crafty way of a man doing the task. If the fellow wants to keep you back, if he has ill feelings to you, he can pile you, he can stubble you down, he can throw his cane on your cane; he can get you checked out. It's a lot of tricks. I can do what we call backing up on the guy. Let us say that I have a partner I did not choose, he line up next to me on a day when I have no partner. I am smarter and faster than he is, and I want to get out of his way; he is keeping me back; he going to become a botheration to me. In order to make things more faster for me, I leave him when I get to a certain place and walk up the row and cut there. If you cut ahead in a cane row you will cause the other man's cane to fall because the wind will blow it over; it not have yours to rest on anymore.

"Sometimes you can account for a row and a half, a row and three quarters, maybe two rows in a day; it all depends on the limits of your physical. Your money is on your cane knife—how you can use it, how agile you are; the ability of the cutter tells the benefit of the row. As you toil, you are learning more better the task; each day more and more. Then you hop up to the big money.

"In the cane field you wears good boots, good safety shoes, and you wears a handguard to keep your hand from getting cut, and you wears a shinguard and you can wear one or two depending on how you know to use your knife. It makes you look a little like a robot, but many a time except for that shinguard some fellows would never go back with good feet. It's a lot of accidents in the fields. Most of your men getting cut. You using the cane knife, a fellow might fall over, and you cut him. It's what we call miscellaneous happenings. I saw a fellow cut another one time in the fields, and that was a grudge, but normally you don't get that. It happens that people get cut, but not in a malice way. In the camps you get a lot of gnashings, and this body don't want to sit next to that body, you get a lot of people walking over each other, but normally you don't get men running one another down with no cane knife in the field. Not to my knowledge.

"The worst thing about the cane field altogether is knowing that you have to make your day. If you are agile, you can make your row. You might not be agile, you make three-quarters. But you make your row and that's a better dollar for your pocket. The only thing to do is to have the faith—faith in God, and faith to take you to the end of the row. And when I reach the end of that row I say, 'Bless God, I made my day.'"

34

One year I went to Florida to observe the end of the season. I spent most of it with a cutter named Turks, from Kingston, who lived at Streamline Camp in Pahokee and whom I had known from Click Farm, and with his friends Cyclops and Screw. Rain had held up the end of the harvest. The cutters tried to guess from the amount of work left when they would be returning to their homes. Even when the harvest is on schedule, the cutters know only approximately when they will be leaving. The companies know the dates they are closing the mills, and are supposed to give the cutters ten days' notice, but often don't let the word out because they don't want any slackening in the cutters' production. The cutters hear this and that. Perhaps a field walker is in the camp office and sees a slip of paper, or overhears a conversation. Because the cutters don't know when they are leaving, they can't let their families know when to expect them. No one meets them at the airport. The ones who live in Kingston share taxis home. Others ride the bus. Sometimes the cutters are given a date, then leave the camp and are held in Miami for a day, perhaps more, until a flight is available. They return to their countries on scheduled flights, so it is a question of a seat's being found.

Screw lived at Streamline with Turks. He had punctured his eardrum with a cane stalk earlier in the season and although it had healed he had found that every time he returned to work his inner ear began to throb and the pain forced him to quit. Cyclops lived at the camp in Belle Glade. Turks and I drove over there one afternoon and picked him up, then went on to Ritta, a U.S. Sugar camp. Turks had heard that the wife of one of the supervisors there was jheri-curling cutters' hair, and the two of them wanted to make appointments. Turks jheri-curled his hair each year at the end of the season. Cyclops, whose given name was Robert, was going to do it for the first time. "I go home looking smashing," he said. "All the girls will say to me, 'Robert, you look smashing.'" In addition, the father of the woman Cyclops lived with in Jamaica worked at Ritta, and Cyclops wanted to say hello. As it turned out, the man wasn't there. Cyclops left a note on his bunk: "We come here but we never see you. We leave Thursday. O.K. Robert." Cyclops placed the note beside a small plaque that read, "The race is not to the swift, nor the battle to the strong." Next to the plaque was a copy of the New Testament called *The Good News*.

From Ritta we drove out past Clewiston to Shawnee so that Turks could pick up some videotapes he was having copied by a man who worked there. He said that he had cut three rows that day. "I was set for it," he said. "I was in a good mood, I was in a spiritual mood, I was in a good mood to go." At Shawnee a group of cutters was standing in front of the house where Turks was picking up the tape. One opened the car door and said to Cyclops, "Of you and your mother, who came first?" A long, impenetrable discussion followed which Cyclops brought to an end by saying, "I was before, and my mother was behind. A man was before a woman. A mother's a woman, I am a man, so I was before my mother. He's got to submit." The other cutters nodded. Turks came out with a copy of *Death Wish 3* and a kung-fu film.

I did not go with Turks when he got his hair jheri-curled. I had done that the year before, when he was living at Click and had arranged with the crew leader's wife to have it done. Their trailer was across the canal from the camp. I watched television while Turks went through the various applications and combings and stylings. A lot of television commercials in south Florida begin with a man standing in front of a car, or with a shoe in his hand, or beside an appliance and saying, "Hello, I'm Frank [or John]." On one commercial a man said, "Men and women, if you're not happy doing what you're doing, stop and learn to drive a tractor-trailer!" Turks sat with his back to the television and held a mirror in one hand so that he could watch the television over his shoulder. A woman came on and said, "Hi, I'm Marlo Bender, can you be thinner? Can you lose weight? Can you reach that perfect dress size?" On the wall was a towel with an image of Jesus. We watched a game show. The host said, "You have a special relative?" and the contestant said, "Yeah, my grandfather was the coinventor of the photo finish at the racetrack and he was the first person to take a picture of a triple dead heat. We have it at our house."

"That must be pretty exciting!"

Turks, with his hair all slicked back, looked like an Apache. On the television a woman said, "I'm a model. I've been working for the major designers in Paris and London, and I have moved back here to have my first baby."

"All right!"

Written in pen on the back of the mirror was, "He is the God of the Second Chance." The camp was full of peddlers hoping to get a piece of the cutters' money. Turks looked out the window and said, "Peddler, peddler, peddler; every minute of the day."

When we got back to the camp we saw that a number of men had done their hair themselves in the bathrooms. They were admiring their images in the mirrors and paying each other compliments. On the next few days they walked around the camp wearing shower caps to keep the dust and the dirt from ruining their hair.

Once he had packed, all that remained for Turks was to sell his gun. Over the last few seasons a number of cutters had been robbed, particularly in Pahokee. One had been robbed on the highway near the camp, and more than a few had begun carrying guns to protect themselves. When Turks bought his he said, "This a gun country, everybody need security." At Streamline, one cutter had shot another by accident. The shooter borrowed the gun and walked out the door of the barracks and pointed it at the fields and pulled the trigger just as the cutter who was hit turned the corner. He took the bullet in his arm. The man with the gun ran inside the barracks, gave the gun back, then ran through the yard of the camp and into the street. Turks saw him there. "He was just walking around, clapping his hands," he said. "You could see the sadness on his face." New Year's Eve Turks and a friend took their guns and some beer to the fields and spent an hour drinking and shooting in the New Year. Turks bought his gun in Pahokee for seventy-five dollars and sold it to a cutter from Barbados for one-forty. The Barbadians are said to be checked less carefully on returning than are the Jamaicans, and Turks didn't want the gun anyway.

One night at the end of a season a few years back, some cutters stuffed cane trash into a shirt and a pair of pants and tied a belt at the waist and a bandanna around the head and fastened a cutlass to one hand and hung a sign on a cord around its neck. The sign said:

"I hear about cutting canes in America, and I leave my home and come here, and now I get here the condition is so rough that I had to run down the Charley's and this is how they have me. Although the crop is finish I still have to come out to see if there anything to do. The White Man Does Steal Us Very Bad."

The cutters set the figure on the porch of one of the cabins and put a water jug beside it. A priest saw it the next morning and took pictures of it. Some time later he asked some white men at the company what they made of it. They said they had consulted an anthropologist who told them that the slogan and the figure had no practical meaning. Probably it had something to do with voodoo. More than likely it was a charm to keep evil away.

Turks had taken up with a woman from Pahokee named Lucy, whom he had met at a bar. By the time I arrived they had been together two months. She had plaited his hair into tiny braids. She used to let him borrow her car and he would sometimes fill it with cutters and drive as far as Palm Beach or Miami just to see what it looked like. I picked him up one night at the camp and we drove down the street past the Streamline Bar and he saw Lucy's car and then Lucy herself standing by a pay phone in the parking lot. She was a short, wide, and formidable figure against the side of a building. Turks likes fat women. He pronounces the word with the soft Jamaican *a*, and almost a second elapses between the *f* and the *t*. He pulled up beside her and introduced us and then got out to talk to her. When he came back to the car he said over his shoulder that he would see her later at home. Lucy said that she wouldn't be there. He said, "Be home," and she said, "*You* ain't home."

Later we went by her house with some fried chicken from Belle Glade. A man there said that Lucy and a friend had walked downtown to the Florida Bar. We drove down there but didn't find her. We went back to the camp and picked up Screw and drove back to Belle Glade and picked up Cyclops and went to the Oasis. A short, fat, damaged-looking white girl absently running a comb through her greasy orange-blond hair came up to Cyclops on the sidewalk and said, "A girl's been asking about you." Cyclops said, "Who?" and the girl said, "Remember that girl you were talking to the other night?" and then she just wandered off into the bar. The four of us drank a beer and drove back to Pahokee and dropped Screw and Turks off, then Cyclops and I went back to Belle Glade. On the way he said that he had a house now. He said that he spent four hundred dollars for the land and twenty-six hundred for the house, which was built of cement from his own design and mostly by himself. He had not seen it finished, though. The last of the work was being done while he was in Florida. He said the house is way out in the country and that his life is easier there than the life Turks leads in town, partly because he grows most of his food. He said that he was very fond of Turks and that if Turks were a woman he would never let him out of his sight. He said that in Jamaica he never hears from Turks. Sometimes he and his girlfriend ride the bus to visit him, but Turks never comes to see them. He stays caught up in his own things in the city. When they leave Florida, Cyclops said, Turks forgets he exists until they come back the next season.

The following afternoon work finished early. Turks and I went to Lucy's house, which amounted to a shack on stilts on a back street in Pahokee. Lucy and three other women were on the porch drinking liquor mixed with Coke and watching their children on the lawn. One of the women was Lucy's sister. She was slim and pretty and slow-moving. She looked at my rental car a moment, then said, "I'd drive that car."

Lucy came down off the porch to talk to us. She was wearing a dress of sheer orange material that clung to her because of her size. Turks touched her backside and she said, "Don't you be petting my ass in front of people. I told you about that." A moment later his hand brushed her chest and she took a swipe at him. They arranged to meet later. The women all seemed a little affected by the drink. The sister sat as still as an Indian and watched her child. Instead of smiling when she was amused, she would look away across the lawn and you could sense the slightest relaxation in her manner.

When we picked Lucy up later a child was crying inside the house. A young girl, Lucy's niece, was on the porch dressed up in blue jeans and a paisley shirt to go to town. Lucy went inside to change out of her housedress. In the meantime Turks played with the children. One of them, a little boy, called him Stepdad. He said, "Who told you to call me that?" The boy said, "No one, I figured it out."

Turks and Lucy and I drove to Click Farm so Turks could say goodbye to the crew leader, who now had another job on the farm. Lucy had never been out there before, she had never been west of Belle Glade. She slept in the backseat most of the way until we left the highway for the fields outside Clewiston and then she stared out the window and eventually she said, "Man you were back out in Nowhere Land." Turks's friend was not at home so we went back to Pahokee. The crop rows spun past the windows. A flock of egrets in the middle of a field stood as still as statues on a lawn and watched us pass. It occurred to me that we had driven nearly forty miles to reach Click Farm and had followed cane fields practically all of the way. "In those fields is a lot of tribulation," Turks said. Lucy was asleep again. "I don't think I will do this anymore," he went on. "It's too much. I been cutting cane for so long I should be able to buy a house. I cannot buy a house. I'm trying my best, but it bend my mind, it break my heart. Sometime when I think about it, I think I'll just go home. I'm on nine seasons straight. I need a Christmas back home."

The next night, Turks's last, Lucy came by the camp to say goodbye. When she arrived Turks was wrapping a blanket around his VCR in order to pack it. Lucy stood outside in the dark and spoke to Turks through a window, half of her face in shadow. Turks invited her in, but she said there were too many men, she wasn't coming in and having their eyes all over her. I went over to say goodbye. She asked if I was coming to their wedding.

I left Turks talking to her and went to find Screw. He had dreamed the night before that he had seen his wife and that she was crying over a dead body, so he was using one of the dream books for gamblers the cutters buy in the supermarkets to predict combinations in the numbers and was looking up crying and seeing a lover and seeing a dead body. He was not going to play, he had no money—he was just passing the time. He was fairly sure that because of the length of his injury and the time he had missed at work he would not be asked back the next season. (He wasn't.) He had seen the advertisement on television of a lawyer from West Palm Beach who he thought might be able to help him get a settlement from the grower for his injury. He said that it had been a very disappointing season for everyone, especially the cutters who had been at Click Farm the year before. They missed it and said they had not realized how good they had had it there. "This camp like some barren ground," he said.

I went back and asked Turks if he was really going to marry

Lucy. He said, "I don't know." I said I had never heard him say that he wanted to live in America. He said maybe for a little while, but only so he could make enough money to go back to Jamaica on better terms. Then he said that he couldn't marry Lucy because she had five children and he would not be able to take care of them properly and anyway his girlfriend and their son in Jamaica were ahead of Lucy in line.

Under the terms of the contracts the cutters sign with the growers a deduction of twenty-three per cent is made from their wages and deposited in savings accounts in their names on their islands. The original purpose of this account was to give the cutters an incentive to return to the Caribbean. The cutters resent being forced to contribute to these accounts. They say it is a dead money that they give, no interest gets on it. The governments of the various islands concerned take the interest. Turks, an exceptionally capable cutter, went home with three hundred dollars, plus about fifteen hundred in the enforced savings account.

35

Caveman called me one morning at the Inn and asked to borrow fifty dollars. He said he hadn't been home in two days and had missed work the day before. He had seen his kids at his mother's house, where he was hiding out, and had told them not to tell their mother where he was. He had been told to report to work that day at twelve, but he wanted to go to a wedding because his girlfriend would be there and he was going to try to make up. He figured that would be a good opportunity because at a wedding everyone is in a good mood.

He came by and picked up the money and we arranged to meet at his trailer that evening and go and find the Barbadian man. When I went there he wasn't around and I didn't see his car anywhere in Harlem, so I went back to my room. The next afternoon I drove out to the fields to meet him. I parked by the other drivers' cars and waited, knowing he would have to show up. I saw Anthony first, who gave me a big wave. When Caveman came in he said he had had trouble with his car the night before. I drove them back to the harvester's office, so they could pick up their paychecks, then into town to cash them, then back to Harlem. Anthony said, "I got the girl for you, Cave."

Caveman said, "Who that?"

"My cousin," Anthony said. "She got green eyes."

Caveman said, "That's the one I want, them green eyes."

"And when she get to *lik*ing somebody," Anthony said, "they turn blue."

Caveman said, "Damn. A woman like that will temptate a man."

I left them off at Anthony's and arranged to come back in an hour. When I returned, no one answered Anthony's door, and the neighbors said they had never heard of him. After I had insisted for some time that I had left him off an hour earlier and watched him go inside, one of them finally said that Anthony was up the street, meaning on the main street of Harlem. When I went up there the drug dealers came off the porches and said 'What you want, I got what you want.' I got back in my car and drove to Caveman's. He was sitting on the stoop waiting for me.

Caveman couldn't remember exactly where the Barbadian lived. We went out of town into the fields. Caveman stopped at a crossroads store and described the trailer off by itself among some fields and the women told us where it was. When we got there no one was home. There was a blue van in the yard and a clothesline crossing the yard with washing hung on it to dry. The trailer had blue shutters and a tattered falling-over lean-to awning on one side. There were pine trees shading it and fields on three sides. There was no one else living within miles. A child's bicycle was turned over in the yard by some stray trash. Caveman said to blow the horn. He wouldn't get out of the car because he said he had seen a pit bull around there once. The trailer was on cinder blocks and from under it came a pregnant mongrel who stood by the car wagging her tail.

I drove Caveman home. He said if I came back at seven we could try the roadhouse again.

A few days before, I had driven past it. In order to get a look at it I planned to go in and ask directions to Click Farm, which was up the road. When I got to the roadhouse, though, the man I knew to be the owner was standing at the head of the driveway. I asked him how to get to Click Farm and he told me. He didn't appear to pay me any mind.

When Caveman and I went back that night I told him I had met the owner and Caveman told me that the man's name was Mr. John. No one else was around when we arrived. Mr. John was by himself in the bar. He is an old black man and he was wearing a white cap, a black shirt with a white abstract pattern, like a drip painting, and dark pants. He was sitting at a table in the middle of the room playing cards by himself. He said he was playing coon cane. All the eights, nines, and tens are dealt out in a pile face up, then a hand of ten is dealt and the game is played something like rummy. Caveman said he would play a hand with him. The television was on with the volume low. I bought Caveman a pint of wine and ordered a bottle of stout. "Stout," Caveman said. "That's what those Jewmaicans drink." The bar had six stools. None matched another. The wine was three-fifty and the beer was a dollar-forty, and Mr. John went to an adding machine in the middle of the bar for the total. He wrapped a napkin carefully around the base of the bottle.

Caveman and Mr. John started to play. Caveman retired a trick. Mr. John said, "You know something about this game?"

Caveman said, "Yeah."

Mr. John said, "That's going to make me tighten up on you."

The room was long and narrow with a white ceiling, and cement walls that were red behind the bar and blue everywhere else. In back of the bar were a mirror and a jar of pickled pig's feet. There were two big posters with calendars on a wall by a pool table. One was "The Great Kings of Africa," and the other "The Great Queens of Africa." Beyond the pool table, where the room was darker, were tables and chairs and a juke box.

Caveman said, "Where all the ladies at?"

Mr. John said, "They ain't around."

Caveman asked how he had come to south Florida.

Mr. John said, "I come down here because my brother-in-law asked for me, sent for me. I said I'd come here for a season. This is 1931. I never went back. Actually I'm getting ahead of myself in my conversation. I did go back from 1936 to 1939, played around, picked apples in Maine, New Hampshire, and Vermont, then came back. I did too good here. I would say every year I had the intention of going back, but when you get in the business you get caught up."

Mr. John dealt a new hand. He said, "I got a bad hand.

I'm pretty good at switching, but I can't do no switching here."

Caveman won two games, then Mr. John stood up abruptly and said, "I'm going to watch 'Sanford and Son' now." He walked over to the bar and stood with his back to us watching the television. We got up and walked over and took stools. In a little while Mr. John said, "How old do you think I am? I'm eighty-one!"

Caveman said, "John, you remember me?"

"I remember your face. Who are your people?"

"James. You remember James that you raised?"

"Oh, yeah, James. James is in trouble, ain't he?"

"Trouble, yeah. He's on probation."

"Probation. Well, that's okay. Long as you don't get on it too much."

He returned his attention to the television. When a commercial came on he said that he used to be a professional gambler, specializing in skin and poker. He said that he would mark his cards with a pin, the tiniest prick on the side of the card to show the value on its face. Once on the right for a jack, once on the left for a queen, and once in the middle for a king. Caveman said that Mr. John was practically unbeatable. Mr. John examined a big diamond he wore on a ring.

Caveman said, "You ever know about Greasy Fat?"

"Yeah."

"He's good at that coon cane."

"You mean that Greasy Fat in Clewiston?"

"Yeah."

"I thought you might be meaning that Greasy Fat in Belle Glade."

He said that if he ever got caught or if a man suspected him he'd just pull out of the game. If a man was on to him from the start he would let that man know he understood, and then they would have to split the take. He said that he prefers to beat a man in the long run. "You don't get greedy," he said. "That's what ruins too many people; they go for the short run."

Caveman said, "What happened to your twin white Cadillacs?"

Mr. John said, "What happened? I got drunk and tore them up. See, I lost my eyesight."

After a moment Caveman asked if there would be any Jamaicans in that night. Mr. John said that he didn't get that many Jamaicans anymore, they seemed worried about catching the AIDS disease. Fewer and fewer people came at all, for that matter.

No one came while we were there. Mr. John lost interest in the television and seemed like he wanted to close up. Caveman said, 'You remember this man?" Mr. John looked at me and said, "Oh, yeah. He asked directions to the Click Farm." Then he turned to me. He said, "You get there all right?"

36

Payday:

"Gentlemen, keep the passes clear, so that when a man getting his money he walk back easy."

"All right, now. Buzzie Gill! Come, come, man, leave the passes open. . . . George Fuller!"

"Yes!"

"Come! Dilton Foster! Sign here. Don't confuse envelopes."

"Elias Ferguson!"

"Ferguson!"

"Write this off, Ferguson, or two you'll get. . . . Come, come, man; the buses be waiting to take you to town. Eliah Blackwell!"

"No Blackwell."

"Calvin Campbell! . . . Moses Zucker!"

"Here!"

"Come and look, man, come and look. . . . Joseph Bruce!"

"Bruce here."

"Connelly! . . . Connelly? . . . Darrell Foster!"

"Yeah, yeah."

"George Thompson!"

"Yes, sir."

"Geoffrey Weir!"

"Yes, yes."

"Leroy Davis!"

"Davis no here, pass it on."

"Come, man, come, come, come. Eustace Francis!"

"Right here."

"Slim!"

"Yes, sir."

"Rupert Smith!"

"Yes, back here."

"Valentine Roy! . . . Calvin Morris!"

"Yes, here Morris."

"God bless you, Morris. . . . Roberts!"

"Yo, yo."

"Come on up! Lawrence!"

"Yes."

"Come on up, Lawrence. . . . Berkeley Johnson! . . . Basil Greer!"

"See Greer."

"Mr. Lie!"

"Right here, man."

"You the ugliest lie I ever see. E. Wright! Mr. Wright!"

"Right here, man."

"Neville!"

"Here Neville."

"Harris! . . . Harris? Any one man see Harris?"

"No Harris."

"Ronald Whyte!"

"He gone to the doctor."

"Let's go, let's go, let's go. Michael Brown, come on up quickly, we got to go. Festus McDonald!"

"That him."

"Sylvester!"

"Here."

"Sylvester this?"

"Yeah."

"Berthram Williams! . . . Carlton Harris! . . . Adolphus Gardner! . . . Levi Harrison! Come on up, man . . . Benjamin Marley! . . . Roy Ballantine! . . . Simon Ashley! . . . Allan MaCreer! Line up, man, let's go, let's go . . . Bertram York! . . . Julius Sullivan! . . . Leroy Dennis!"

"Yes, man."

"Knowles! Mr. Knowles! Come, come, man, hurry . . . Kenneth Gordon! Gordon!, let's go. . . . Peter James! . . . Nathan Nelson!"

"Look Nelson."

"Grantley Robertson! . . . Connelly! . . . Where Connelly?"

"Him gone, send me come tell you."

"Tell Connelly him pay at the office. Nelson St. Ray! . . . Peter Ishmael! . . . Augustus Irwin! . . . Nathaniel Gordon! . . . Lazarus Stewart! . . . Alwyn Greer! . . . Reginald Allen! Hurry, man. I announce it, you come. David Baptist! . . . Baptist!"

"Here Baptist."

"Take your envelope, Baptist. That it man. Let's go."

37

As a rule, growers rest a field every five years. Most farms are arranged so that approximately twenty per cent of their land lies fallow each season. Before replanting, growers often flood a field to rid it of parasites; to kill insects, a field needs to lie under water for at least seven days. Flooding also halts the oxidation of the soil. Growers sometimes double-crop fields they are resting from cane, usually planting rice. Growers with cattle sometimes grow feed corn, which is planted at the end of January and is a hundred-and-twenty-day crop. The field is then disked for weeds until August when it is planted with cane. A cover crop like cow peas slows subsidence, plus returns nitrogen to the soil. Rice grows on flooded fields, which leaves them clean of weeds. It does not draw any parasites (corn attracts stalk borers and wireworms), and the return from the two crops it supplies pays for the flooding and delivers a profit. This return, added to the income from the last ratoon of the field, might make it worth a grower's while to squeeze one more harvest from a field, thus lowering planting costs.

Many people who object to the way the sugar industry conducts its business say that the growers should give up their government support and raise other crops. Often these people suggest vegetables. The market for winter vegetables, however, is saturated; even a hundred more acres contributing, say, lettuce might disrupt it. Moreover, many vegetables do not thrive on muck soil. Tomatoes grown on muck tend to be watery and to taste as if they had taken on an abundance of some aspect of the soil, say, copper, which is added through fertilizers. Raise citrus then, people say. Muck soil, because it is bacterial, contains a number of elements harmful to citrus, particularly root diseases. Also, it does not drain well. Citrus likes a dry field. Also, some people believe that citrus ripens too fast on muck. Others say this is not true, but what happens is the grower of citrus on muck gets a fruit that tends to bruise easily and be watery and taste insipid. Muck might produce a softball-sized orange, but there would be little inside it but seeds.

Here's what the growers might try: catfish ponds. Sell the topsoil to gardeners on the coast, dig a forty-acre pond in the field, raise catfish, two, three years walk away a millionaire. People on the west coast of the lake do it. Something else: grow ramie. This is a fibrous plant grown during the Second World War (on land now deep in cane) to substitute for hemp in the making of rope. Something else: attempt to retrieve starch from potatoes. This was done (without success) by U.S. Sugar also during the Second World War. Grow nursery trees, or sod, or raise cattle—two or three cows an acre. Grow field corn. Flood the fields and grow rice. None of these will even really pay taxes on the land or return growers anything like the fine, fine, superfine living they have known with sugar.

38

Caveman said he knew a man who had been burned in a cane fire and I asked if he could introduce me. I went to his trailer one evening to pick him up. He was sitting on the couch in the living room, with his shirt off, putting on his shoes. He had just woken up. His girlfriend was in the room with a small boy and a tall, pretty woman about forty, her mother. The woman was sitting on the arm of the couch and watching her daughter fold laundry. Caveman paused in putting on his shoe and looked at her and said, "Mother-in-law, I've been thinking about you all day. What's your name?"

The woman said, "Shirley."

Caveman said, "Shirley, yeah."

The woman said, "Good things or bad?"

"Good, pretty good."

We picked up Anthony at his new apartment above a bar on the main street of Harlem. He said, "Place I live now is *safe*. You try to break in there and people going to hear your *foot*prints. And you try to break the lock on that door and that going to make some *noise*."

Anthony was wearing a baseball cap with a pair of sunglasses resting above the visor. I asked Caveman if he would drive, since I didn't know where we were going. He settled himself behind the wheel and said, "I don't know why you let me drive all the time, many wrecks as I've had."

We found the man on Main Street, standing outside Betty's New Suite Inn, next to a piece of graffiti that said,

Sheri # one girl

He got into the car and Caveman introduced him by his last name, Fluellen. He was tall and thin and had a face with smooth shiny copper-colored skin and high cheekbones. He looked as if he had Indian blood. He said he had no work at the moment but hoped to get a job driving a tractor for one of the growers. He had a gap between his two top teeth and was missing a tooth below it. He wore a wool cap and under it his hair was long and braided.

Fluellen said, "This was in February 1981, I think it was about the twenty-third, somewhere around there. It was down at the Power Line Road, and it was burning the last two forty-acre blocks in that field. I was a harvester but I had to burn that day. We burned the south side and walked up the west and the part we burned first burned up faster than the part I burned last, and the man in the truck who was picking us up when we finished pulled up and told me to get on the truck, and we went back up the field to the other end and it got hotter and hotter and the wind was pushing real real hard, and it got so hot it was unbearable, and I guess in a blind rage I couldn't stand it, and when we got to the headland I stood up in the bed of the truck, and the heat was so intense that it caught my shirt on fire, and you know how the machines tear up the road, rut it all up, and the fire pinned the truck a moment, then it started bouncing in all the ruts and the flames was hitting the hood of the truck and bouncing up off it and splashing like the fire was water, then the truck got going faster, and the road was rough and with all of this rage I felt myself falling off the truck, and to keep from falling on my head I did a little spin and it rolled me about fifty feet and broke my collarbone. The man driving the truck probably didn't even know Fluellen was gone—they ride with the air conditioning on—I imagine when he look back in the truck he say, 'Where Fluellen?' As soon as I stopped rolling I jumped into the big ditch, I was thinking water, water, water, and it sure felt soothing, Lord it sure did, and when I came out I was just asking, 'Why me? Why Fluellen? On the last two blocks of that field?' The man had stopped the truck and him and his partner came up and touched me and I screamed so loud I scared them. They jumped back and they pulled my skin right off me.

"They put me in the ambulance and took me to the Lee Memorial Hospital in Fort Myers. When I got to there all I had of my shirt was the collar and the cuffs. I stayed two and a half months. They didn't do any skin grafts because I didn't want that, I figured with enough time my anatomy could take care of it. It about sweetened up my face, though."

Fluellen's eyes were cloudy and moist and the color of tea and he looked like he hadn't slept in a while. He sat straight up in the backseat and stared ahead and held his hands in his lap.

Anthony said, "What about them other dudes?"

Fluellen nodded. "Two days before I got burned there was two other guys working for U.S. Sugar and they got burned and they weren't so fortunate," he said. "One of them died. They were running the water wagon. Driving the tractor and they run right into a ditch they didn't know was there. You know the wind can change on you and come into another field, the fire jumped and they were out there to beat it down so the fire didn't spread and I think they might have panicked. Ran into the field and got lost in the cane and didn't know which way they were going. Got burned up like wild hogs. You can jump into the water wagon but they didn't. I heard it burned the dead man's shoes right off his feet."

Caveman nodded. Anthony said, "How the person gets burned up is the fire must draw the breath right out of him. *Stun* him. One time I saw a rabbit run right into the flame and stop dead like he *froze*."

Fluellen turned and looked out the window. He looked at his hands folded in his lap then he looked back out the window.

"You see," he said, "I don't know whether this is what motivated me or not but this place had an abundance of wildlife." He paused and looked sideways at Caveman. "Now this is going to make Caveman laugh," he said, "and this is going to make Anthony laugh when I tell them." He took a cigarette from his pocket and tapped it down. Caveman started to laugh and Anthony started laughing too. Fluellen lit his cigarette. Caveman said, "Yeah, I know what you're saying. Tell him what that wildlife was."

Fluellen blew smoke into the air and looked at his image in the window. He touched a spot on his cheek. Then he looked at Caveman.

"See, he wanted a raccoon so he could barbecue it," said Caveman.

Fluellen shook his head. "But that coon come out and see me he say, 'That nigger was going to barbecue me, look like he the one got barbecued.'"

By the time they stopped laughing the windows were fogged. Caveman wiped the mist off his and stared out with a certain concentration, as if he were thinking of something important. Fluellen snuffed his cigarette. Then he stretched. Then he sat quietly. Then he said, "You about ready to slip away, Cave?" and Caveman said, "Yeah, I'm ready."

39

A Jamaican:

"They call me House, since in Jamaica we play a lot of card games in my home and every sixth hand I take a dollar from the pot, because my light is burning. This cutting cane is like a trade for me, like a carpenter or a mason, or an engineer. I'm a veteran at it. When I return to Jamaica I got nothing else to go with, then sugar cane time come, I journey back here. In Jamaica I'm a poor man, I'm a pauper. In America everyone can afford a house and a car. I have no car. I can build no house. In America you can sit there and the next day you will be a millionaire because of that game 'Chance of a Lifetime,' that we watch on TV. In Jamaica we don't have that, it more harder in Jamaica.

"In America we work the roughest way to make a living. Coming over they ask if you're willing to work seven days a week, willing to wash your own clothes, willing to eat poor, willing to obey, work in all style of weather, eat rice seven days. We take eye test, hands test, feet test; they test the entire structure to show you are perfect. When we going home don't you think they should give us a test? Going home we get no test; whatever time you go home with some pain from the contract you must spend from your pocket to mend it. The food they never fix properly. Too many men to cook for, too much hurry to get that food fixed. Sometime they cook that rice all night. The meat one time it was spoiling; it stink. Bossman don't need cook, he need men to cut his cane. If I complain he carry hatred for me.

"A lot of accident happen in the cane. When you working, your hand is sweaty, maybe the bill slip and fly up, maybe take your hand or your foot. Maybe take your partner. Sometimes cane fly up and lick me in the mouth; call that fly-up cane. You mash up your back from the never-ending turning and bending. Your hand become like part of a machine; look at my palm, the bill rest here; it make a channel for its shape. When you go home, that one hand you have been cutting with you can't use. It's no good for anything else; you got to use the other one until it heal. Whatever time you are working in the cold, you feel it right up your arm to your heart. If a piece of cane hit you then, it is terrible. First camp I go to in 1979 I see a big man cry from the cold and they had to take him back to the camp. All day we breathing the soot and ash from the fields. Our lives one day shorter for each day we cut cane.

"We complain but only to one another. We know it hard and you got to survive. God is with us, we take him with us day by day, we got to work with him, we got to watch dangerous things—snake, bobcat, ants climbing up your pants' leg to sting you, the cane stalk strike you in your eye, pierce your eardrum. Sometime to make money we got to eat no lunch, we got no time for it, sick and still working. Maybe you sick and you go to a doctor but he say go and try it, and you must, because otherwise they say you refuse your work. Racing, we get chop. You got to be wise and understand yourself and be quiet, otherwise they send you home. It is very disappointing, the way we are treated. We are slaves. They pay us money, but really they buy us. Our government sell us to the contract. We live in captivity, we must obey our master, anything he say we have to do. For we it is rough. We have always a struggle. We are all of us under a sufferation.

"When I lie in the bed and look back home, I look at my wife and I feel so disappointed. I want to see her now. Whatever time I in the field, I wish she could see me there. Sometimes we lie on the bed and say something like 'Joe Grind, he pick your apple,' or we getting a letter and we say Joe Grind writing us for money. Joe Grind is at home jumping up on your bed and taking his cap and backhanding your son, saying, 'Go away.'

"Returning back home it is strange, the separation we have passed through, great tribulation. You become a foreigner because you are away so much. Most people like experience and travel but that wear off. It is lonely being away. Right now I feel lonely. Sometimes at night, nature just kill me."

40

The last time I saw Caveman he said he had run into Noel, his Barbadian friend, the night before in Harlem and Noel had said he would talk to me and had told Caveman where he worked and that we should pick him up at the end of the day. Noel worked for the water management company. At a store Caveman asked directions from a man who was holding a jug of distilled water by its handle with the thumb of his right hand. He had no other fingers on that hand. Caveman called him Six. When we drove off Caveman said, "The first time I saw Six was in a bar. He asked for some credit and they call him Six and I said, 'Why did you call him that?' "

I asked about Star Child and Caveman said that the first time he had seen Star Child, at a club in Belle Glade, Star Child had been wearing a diaper. He said it was part of an act, for publicity. We passed some canals, and Caveman said that in order to swim in them people would study them first for gators. He said you could see gators because they part the surface of the water just slightly, like a fish, but big. He said that anyway they only strike from the top.

When we arrived at the water management company, about three-thirty, there were six men playing basketball on a fenced-in court inside the parking lot. Noel was watching. He came over to us, and said he couldn't leave until the bossman, who was playing, did. Caveman said he used to love playing basketball. He said that he had been at college on a football scholarship but had given it up. "My head be all the time hurting up," he said. "Had to keep the aspirin bottle with you. Those guys that hitting you be three hundred and ten pounds and moving at fifteen, twenty miles an hour. I called up my mamma and said I was coming home. That be too much." As soon as the bossman left and was out of sight everyone else started his car and left too.

At Noel's we sat on the steps of his trailer. It was hot and he wore his shirt open. He had a scar in the center of his chest, on the breastbone. He said that a woman had stabbed him. He was living with her and she saw him out with another woman and when he came home he walked in the door and she jumped out of a closet and planted the knife in him. He stepped back outside and down the steps and into his car and drove to the hospital with the knife stuck there. He said he had also been shot twice by women, and then he showed me a scar on his shoulder where the mark left by the four tines of a fork planted in his shoulder by a woman showed plainly, like a little constellation.

Out in the fields a loader collected the day's harvest. Noel said that he had been hired to manage this farm and given the trailer to live in, but the farm had failed, so he was looking for another place closer to town. What he told me about cutting sugar cane I pretty much already knew, but it was pleasant sitting on his porch and looking out over the fields.

When we got back to Harlem, Caveman wanted to check the street. "Let me see what the night be like," he said. "I can always tell by this time of the afternoon how the night shaping up."

By Betty's New Suite Inn, a man stepped from the curb and yelled to Caveman. We turned around and went back and got him. He said he had driven a tractor for one of the growers until earlier in the week, when he had overturned a wagon and got fired. Caveman saw his girlfriend pass in her car and we followed her until she pulled into the driveway of a trailer several lots from Caveman's. He got out and went to see if he could talk her into giving up the car for the night. He came back a few moments later saying that in exchange she had wanted him to accompany her to the wash house to do laundry and then go shopping for food. "I don't go shopping with no woman," he said. "I did it one time. I didn't *like* it."

We drove back toward Main Street. Caveman said, "I got to get me a new piece of car. I wrecked my last one."

"I remember that," his friend said.

"Time before that took me five years to get a new one."

"Damn."

"You know Charles?"

"Tall dude from Belle Glade?"

"Hang out up on the street there?"

"Yeah. Always wearing that hat?"

"That the one."

"Charles."

"They say he's crazy."

"Word up."

"You see what he's driving?"

"Check it out."

"Brand-new."

"Where'd he get all that money?"

"Being crazy," said Caveman.

"Check it out, man. Charles."

"Maybe I ought to go that road," Caveman said."

"You probably wouldn't have to go that far if you took it," said his friend.

41

An issue of the fashion tabloid *W* from February of 1987 contains an article about a family named Fanjul, who own the Okeelanta Corporation and the Osceola Corporation, and whose fortune the writer estimates as being at least five hundred million dollars. The article bears a dateline from Palm Beach. It includes the information that the two oldest brothers in the family are named Alfonso and José. Alfonso, called Alfie, is married to a woman named Tina, and José, called Pepe, is married to Emilia. Tina is quoted at lunch on the patio of her home. Palm trees are in view. Also a butler wearing white gloves and gray and black livery. Crista, her daughter, describes a ritual having its origins in the behavior of her ancestor José Gomez-Mena, a sugar baron:

> "He walked into a Havana cafe, ordered an espresso and filled his cup three-quarters full of

> sugar. The cafe owner shrugged and said, 'Who do you think you are . . . Señor Gomez-Mena?' Nowadays, when we go to a restaurant or a diner, we do something very similar. We each open about five or six packets of sugar and pour them out into our saucers."
>
> Everyone laughs. A little frivolous waste for tradition's sake is relished as charming.

Accompanying the article are photographs: a handsome dark-haired woman in a silk print dress, seated with a small dog on a chintz sofa in a room with many objects ("Tina Fanjul and Tai," according to a caption); two cabin cruisers, one of them equipped for sport ("The houseboat for guests and a fishing boat"); three figures having lunch at a table in a garden, attended by a man in a white jacket and dark trousers ("Allan Ryan Sr., Tina Fanjul and Bobbie Ryan"); a corner of a house surrounded by shrubs, with a lawn in the foreground ("The spacious lawns around Alfie and Tina Fanjul's home"); a family portrait; a white house under a blue sky ("The Pepe Fanjuls' new home"); another woman in a room with a dog (Emilia Fanjul and Heather"); a library with chintz-covered couches and drapes and many objects, as well as a few books ("The library in Tina and Alfie Fanjul's home"); and a young woman seated on a hammock with a different dog ("Christa Fanjul and Bumpa").

Emilia and Pepe live in a twenty-six-room house which belonged to a man whose family supplied arms to the Germans during World War II. Pepe drives a red Ferrari. Alfie has a blue Mercedes, with "AF" on the license plates. Pepe is a former president of the Florida Sugar Cane League. He also wanted to be president of Cuba. The family has lunch together every Sunday, occasionally on fish caught among reefs that Alfie has had built beneath his dock on Lake Worth. Formal dinners at his house are served on a table made from the skins of goats and boars and finished to a gloss. On such occasions it is the family's habit to burn candles hand-dipped by monks.

The article also mentions that the family's companies recently paid a fine of eighty-five thousand dollars to the Environmental Protection Agency for violating federal air pollution standards, and that the family recently reneged on a promise made by Gulf + Western when that company had owned Okeelanta to exchange lands in the Everglades restoration area (which would then be preserved) for other state lands.

42

I often think of Turks in his house. It is so small. It is one room. It is hot and dark. To obtain privacy, in order, say, to leave his bed in the morning and dress, he turns his back on Paulette, his girlfriend, and Robert, their son, who is seven and shares the bed with them. In Jamaica it is not unusual to live in quarters so restricted.

Turks's house is in Kingston, among a number of small houses forming a settlement beside a road leading into the hills. Between the houses and the road is a culvert for carrying rainwater to the sea. At the head of the dirt road entering the settlement is a tavern—a bar with a couple of stools. Beyond the tavern, on the left-hand side, the culvert; on the right, a low wall, then a break of several feet forming an entrance to a yard, then a higher wall, part of a structure that has been abandoned. The yard is common to several houses. Nothing is growing there; the dirt is packed hard, like a floor; where it passes their doorways the women sweep it clean. The houses are made from cement and finished with plaster mixed with sand. They are built on sloping ground; some are higher than others, a number share walls. On one of the walls a person has written: "Sad Christmas, No Money." Sheets of tin form the roofs. Rocks and cinder blocks hold the tin against the wind. By the entrance to the small courtyard Turks shares with his neighbors is a shade tree with a root that has been exposed by erosion. This is a gathering place. Over time the haunches of the people who have sat there have polished the root to the texture of finished wood, like a piece of furniture.

Cats lie in the sun. Women dry sorrel on tables for tea. Dogs forage in the culvert. Goats stray into the road beside the settlement. When cars run them down the owners can't collect damages because the goats aren't supposed to be loose. There are no lights in the yard; the darkness at night is complete.

Turks's house has doors on two sides. When someone is home the doors stand open for a breeze. Around the door frames are holes in the plaster plugged with pages of the *Daily Gleaner*, Jamaica's newspaper. At the head of the bed is a curtain draped in a circle about the size of a tire which serves to conceal clothes and the suitcases Turks takes nearly empty to Florida.

In his house are one bed, a stove and refrigerator bought in Clewiston, a table with an oilcloth and a couple of chairs, a sideboard of stained wood that has on it a television (also from Clewiston), a VCR (bought secondhand in Moore Haven from a woman who jheri-curled Turks's hair one year and whose husband cooked at Click Farm), and a pair of ceramic collies from the Coronation Market, an outdoor market in downtown Kingston; Turks is fond of figurines. Around the television screen he has strung small colored lights. The floor is covered with painted tiles. The ceiling is low and made from canvas. It is not possible to walk three steps in any direction without meeting an obstacle.

In the evening children often come to the back door to watch movies and because Turks gives them parts of his meal.

Turks carries water from a pump in the yard. There is no sink in his house. He washes dishes, washes himself, removes the plate from his mouth and scrubs it, in view of his neighbors.

In yards nearby are vines bearing pumpkins and yams, as well as trees that bear coconuts, bananas, ackee (ackee and salt fish is a popular Caribbean breakfast), pawpaw, guinnap, guava, avocado, two kinds of mangoes (Bombay and Kitney), breadfruit, nesberry, custard apple, and star hopper. The arrangement of their planting is accidental and they bear without being maintained.

The tenants rent their houses by the month. Because many cannot raise the sum all at once, the landlord visits weekly. He comes on Sunday. In Jamaica this kind of landlord is called a Sunday landlord.

In the country, people build stands beside the roads and display the produce of the area, or sell drinks. The stands are the simplest kind of structures, with no elaboration, unless it is to have a counter or some shelves. Sometimes on a road there will be nothing but scenery for miles, then a stand, with a few coconuts and a woman's face behind the counter (the eyes cast down, or to the side, or meeting yours as you pass), then nothing again for miles; sometimes there are five or six stands in a row, each selling oranges, or mangoes, or breadfruit, or Red Stripe beer. At night most of the stands are empty. At some the proprietors light rags stuffed in Mason jars filled with kerosene and place them on the counter. A woman sews, a man reads to some children by the light from the flame.

In Jamaica I watched women fan themselves and raise the hems of their skirts to wipe the sweat from their faces. A buzzard cruised scrawny cattle in a field. At Raphael's Cooling Spot a man on a stool looked out at the traffic passing and listened to the radio announcer's account of a soccer game taking place in England. A child played by the road with a toy: a car made from a milk carton with wheels made from limes. Women wearing bright colors left the brassiere factory in Bailey's Vale at the end of the day and walked home under the trees on both sides of the road, like a procession. A baby wrapped in a blanket slept on a chair in the shade of the overhang on a porch. On the arm of the chair a Bible lay open to Job, where the baby's mother had been reading before she heard voices in the yard next door and went to see what was happening.

In valleys by the ocean I passed fields divided by hedges with red flowers. Turks said they were called shueblack flowers and that farmers use them to fence land when they haven't got the money for wood and nails and wire. Rounding a curve outside Port Maria we smelled the sea. Jamaican fishermen believe that when you can smell the sea it's got plenty fish. Women washed clothes in a river and laid them on rocks to dry, so that from the road high above the arrangement of colors on the riverbank looked like a pattern worked in a rug. At a stand by the water near Port Antonio I watched a young girl serve parrotfish fried in oil to a tourist and his girlfriend in a sports car. When they left, the girl woke a dog sleeping under one of the tables and fed him the bones.

I drank beer on the porch of a house in the country being built by a cutter I know. The house is not quite completed. The cutter was in Massachusetts picking apples. Between apples and sugar cane he is away nine months of the year. While he is gone, his girlfriend plants fruit trees and flowers in the yard, so that the place always looks different to him when he returns. In the morning she washes her face with soap from a department store in Clewiston. At night she watches television, on a set bought in Belle Glade. She thinks that television has made her life in the country bearable. She thinks that watching television is like meeting new people every night.

A man wearing a uniform with epaulets and decorations like medals and walking a German shepherd on a leash patrolled the parking lot of the hotel where I stayed. Returning at night through the blocks approaching the hotel, I drove through a gauntlet of whores hissing at me from the sidewalks.

Because I said I thought Jamaican women were handsome, Turks took me to a club in the city where two black women wearing bathing suits danced on a platform in back of the bar. I walked up to the bar to buy beer. The women danced under red and green lights. Sometimes they would turn their backs to the audience: a couple dancing, Turks, a woman he knew whom he had seen on the street and invited to join us, his niece Karen, and a neighbor, Densil. When I got back to the table with the beers the woman with Turks said, "If you were to be with one of them, they would break your back." More people arrived. The woman danced a long time with Densil, then sat in a chair against the wall with her dress halfway up her thigh. When we left two men followed us out of the club and into the parking lot and asked Karen and the woman if they wanted to stay. Then we went to the woman's house, the first real house I had been to in Kingston. It was among a row of houses in a development. It didn't seem finished. It was hot inside, the air was still, and there were bars on all the windows. The woman said that St. Martin's was the best place in the Caribbean. She said that it was "totally benz." Turks asked if I understood what she was talking about. I said no. He said that she meant that everyone drove a Mercedes-Benz. Karen mixed rum and whiskey in a tall glass. She said it would make her sexy. She passed out in a few minutes. Then the woman's husband came home. He was tired. He went upstairs without really saying much and then we left. On the way home I asked Turks what the man did that made him enough money to have a house and he said he was a policeman. Then I took Karen and Turks and Densil home and drove back to my hotel past the whores making sounds like waves falling back on a beach.

. . .

I went with Turks one day to visit his sister in the hills above Oracabessa, on the northern coast. She had a small store in the basement of her house and she made us lunch from things that I bought from her. I sat on her porch looking out over the tops of the trees to the ocean. In the middle of the yard across the way two little girls finished hanging out wash then began dancing to reggae music coming from inside the house. They were rolling their hips in circles and grabbing their crotches and looking over their shoulders to see if I was watching. If they met my eyes, they collapsed in laughter. Each was wearing a white party dress; one had a tear in the skirt. Storm clouds rolled in from the sea, the air cooled; at the first drops of rain the girls shrieked and ran to the lines for the wash. Driving home in the rain, we passed schoolgirls waiting for the bus. Since there was no shelter they stood where they were and got soaked to the skin. Their uniforms stuck to their bodies, outlining their tall, gangly forms. A woman at a stand selling mangoes sat hunched under the counter, beneath her leaking roof. On the counter the mangoes were washed clean and shiny by the rain.

Several hours of each day I spent as a passenger. It was important to Turks always to go from one place to another in the least amount of time. Many of the roads we traveled were narrow and built on the sides of mountains, with sharp curves. "Nothing like this in your country, where you go around corners and you can't even see the road!" he once said. There were always more people on the roads than there were cars, so that coming around the sharpest turn, with nothing but a complete change of life on one side of the car, we might find a herd of goats in our lane, or a bus avoiding a herd of goats, or children. Sometimes a tree or rocks that had come loose in the rain. We drove through whole towns with people in them doing nothing more complicated than watching us pass. I saw a man holding a child by the side of the road flinch and clench the child to his breast at the speed of Turks's approach. In Castleton Gardens two girls hopped up on a stone wall to get out of his way; the wind from the car stirred their skirts. Another time I saw the draft from our passing ruffle the feathers on the back of a chicken and flatten a man's collar against the back of his neck. I expected someone to come after us for the way Turks drove until I realized that the sight of a driver like Turks fireballing through town scaring up poultry and scattering livestock was the kind of event people were sitting beside the road waiting for.

I went with Turks to the Coronation Market, in Kingston. He parked in front of Gimme de Break Boutique, which was closed, its windows shuttered, and went looking for a man who owed him money for a watch. In the center of the market is a huge open-sided shed with a tin roof; underneath it vendors sell from stalls or handcarts. A man stood beside an upright barrel on the end of which he had laid out tripe and waved off flies with a rolled newspaper. Next to him sat a woman beside a table on which were old rum bottles filled with root juices the color of tea. Next to her, baskets made from wicker; next to that, bananas; next to that, yams, limes, and scallions; next to that, red peas; next to that, custard apples; next to that, plantains; next to that, pig's tails; next to that, red corn and cucumbers; next to that, fish that were blue and red and laid out on top of barrels in the shade; next to that, more tripe; next to that, salted fish; next to that, molasses, honey, and olive oil in old rum bottles on tables covered with newspaper; next to that, more roots; next to that, teas, rice bitters, dried soup, and chicken feet.

Outside, around a square of low, flat-roofed buildings with fantails and false pediments, painted in bright colors but a while ago, women were selling from handcarts or from trays balanced on boxes. On the trays were arrangements of vegetables—three tomatoes beside three tiny peppers beside fifteen small onions—next to rows of spices gathered in small plastic bags closed with a piece of wire, or in piles shaped like cones. There was no breeze. The women squatted with their knees splayed and drew their skirts up between their legs, like diapers. Against the sun at their backs they opened up cardboard boxes and wore them like hats, the flaps spread over their shoulders and backs, the front edge resting on the top of their foreheads. Or held umbrellas. They made change from the pockets of their aprons without standing up or sometimes even looking at the person they were dealing with, they just held their hands above their heads and the person took his money from their palms. Turks found the man who owed him, but he had broken his arm the day before in a fall and was in pain and Turks decided not to ask for the money, although he could have used it and the man had owed him for some time. On the way back to the car he bought soursap, a fruit, from a woman who handed him a scale with a basket and told him to weigh it. Then he bought a pineapple to squeeze for its juice.

At a storefront butcher just off the square, a line on the sidewalk led through the door and ended in front of two small windows, like betting stalls at a racetrack. What was left for sale was written by hand on sheets of paper taped to the walls and the windows: pig trotters, pig heads, turkey necks, chicken backs, local mutton, beef liner, goat head, and tripe. Turks bought cow skin, which we had boiled that night for dinner.

Above the square and the old-fashioned buildings, buzzards rode the currents of heat.

A few weeks before I arrived Turks had been walking the road through the settlement when he heard Paulette shrieking. A letter had arrived for him from America, with the address written in a woman's hand. Paulette opened it. "And she write to my house!" she was screaming. Everyone agreed it was an outrage to write Turks at their home. Turks turned the corner and went up the street and stayed away two nights and one day, until she calmed down.

43

Few Americans apply to cut sugar cane. People who live in south Florida know about the danger and the drudgery of the task and are mostly not interested and few who live outside the area would ever know the opportunity existed. By the terms of the arrangements through which the industry obtains West Indian cutters, the growers are required to make jobs available first to American citizens and legal aliens. When the growers have satisfied the Department of Labor that an insufficient number applied, they can request foreign cutters based on the estimates of the tonnage in their fields. In considering the requests, the Department of Labor assumes that a man cuts one ton of cane per hour. The growers are hostile toward American applicants and protective of the supply of West Indian cutters, who, in addition to being skilled, form a labor force that is docile; labor difficulties of any seriousness the growers solve by shipping home the discontented cutters. Atlantic Sugar Growers sent home three hundred cutters during a strike in 1982. In 1986 Okeelanta sent home three hundred and fifty. The trouble began in a field one morning three weeks into the season over a row price so low the ticket writers would not give it out. The cutters had been discouraged by the prices all season; some had cut the same fields in seasons past for better money and felt that the situation was dire and not going to improve. They left the field and went into other fields asking cutters to stop working. The liaison officers arrived and said they would try to negotiate a price, but the cutters would have to return to work while they were doing it. Some did; most began walking back to the camp. Work was called off and the rest of the cutters were rounded up and taken back to the barracks. The next morning the buses were late. Some cutters stood on the lawn waiting for them or talked to the liaison officers, others stayed in the barracks. At some point, a vice president of the company came out of the camp office, spoke to some people who worked for him, and returned to the office. Moments later the Belle Glade police arrived, as well as deputies from the Palm Beach County Sheriff's Office, as well as troopers from the Florida Highway Patrol, as well as canine officers with dogs, as well as an ambulance. A number of cutters ran into the barracks. Some of the police pointed shotguns at the cutters, who saw the ambulance and the dogs, and thought they were going to die. The dogs were let loose in the barracks. Two cutters were bitten; one was arrested. The police began loading cutters from the lawn and others who had fled the barracks onto the buses. No one told them where they were going. Some figured out they were not headed for the fields and went out the emergency exits at the back of the buses and kept on traveling and never returned to the camp. Seven buses, some of them driven by policemen, took the three hundred and fifty cutters to the Florida Fruit and Vegetable Association headquarters in Hialeah. There a number of cutters asked for their jobs back, saying they were never part of the strike but were just waiting in the barracks when the dogs arrived and were herded in with everyone else and forced onto the buses. They were refused. Over the course of the next three days, as room could be found, the cutters were sent home on commercial flights. Hardly anyone had been able to bring anything with him from the camp; there had been no time. At some point during the three days a van showed up at the Association's headquarters and dumped a collection of cutters' belongings on the lawn, through which the cutters sorted, each hoping to find something of his own. Some cutters had no shoes; most were wearing only their work clothes. Humiliation is what they felt at returning home with no money and with nothing to show for the time in America, which had once held such promise. People at the airport gave them money to take buses and get something to eat. The Jamaican television station filmed some of them arriving; one man I spoke to in Jamaica a few months later told me that he had got back to his house and heard from his friends that they had seen him on television. Because of the shotguns and the numbers of policemen wearing helmets and visors and the dogs and the atmosphere of war, the cutters in describing the events of the strike refer to the Okeelanta camp as the Vietnam Camp.

. . .

During the December of 1982, the Department of Labor notified the Mississippi state employment office that jobs were available cutting sugar cane in Florida, the people at the employment office said they had candidates, and the Department of Labor had the sugar industry send someone to Mississippi to explain the work and interview anyone interested. One hundred and seventy-seven men, two of them white, signed up, were checked out, and boarded buses on December 17 for the twenty-four-hour ride to south Florida. After a little more than two weeks, one hundred and seventy-six had quit or been fired.

(Men I will call) Emlen, Oscar, William, and Thomas, from Mississippi:

"What I remember, I had gone to the unemployment service looking for work and there was none." (Emlen) "Either I was overqualified or it was a job I didn't really want. The man at the Veteran's Council called me up and said that the representative of the sugar company was going to come get guys to cut sugar cane in Florida, so I went to the place and the representative was there, and they were letting in only so many people at a time, because the building wasn't really big enough for the people that wanted to get in to cut sugar cane. Inside the man was talking about all the things that would happen while we were in Florida, the equipment we would be using. They told us that it was going to be some hard work. I never ran away from no hard work in my life. I looked at hard work as a way to keep myself in shape. Some of the other things that he told supposed to be to our advantage: we would be in a camp that had pool tables, basketball courts, that if someone got hurt there would be a nurse on duty twenty-four hours a day, we would be paid minimum wage for eight days and then we'd go to four sixty-nine an hour. It was told to us also from the beginning, if any of us don't make the training period we had to pay our way back, and the food in the camp would be five-fifty a day. He told us the most nationality there was in the camp, that would be the type of food we would be eating. They gave us a physical; get your weight, get your height, tell you to void in a cup, okay, you void in a cup, the doctor comes in and checks your lungs, and that was it."

"The bus left that morning and get there the next day." (Thomas) "Some dudes wanted to bring their cars. They told you you don't need to bring no car. They told you you'd be around a lot of quicksand. They said if you wanted to go into town, they would take you. As we were coming into the Glades area it was early morning. I saw nothing but sugar cane plants everywhere, like a jungle. My first impression was, *Wow, we are in a desert place.* We were watching the Jamaicans arriving in the cane fields. There were already some cutting. We didn't even look to see how they were doing it, because we didn't know that what it was we were looking at was what we would be doing. Most of the guys on the bus drunk anyway from the bus stopping at liquor stores all the way from Mississippi. Only thing I noticed was when them Jamaican dudes come back at the end of the day they looked real bad. That had cause to stop me to think that something was awfully wrong at that camp. I said, 'I *know* that's hard.'"

"When we got off the bus at the reception place, we don't see nothing but Jamaicans." (Oscar) "The company man told us to stand outside this building and they would call us. The group I was in was called in finally and they told us then that we were going to have to work pretty hard. They said any man that think he can't bend down and get on his knees and use a mercedes, what they call the cane knife, better withdraw his application. The contracts were on the table, and a couple of people picked it up to read it, and the man said, 'Well, you don't really need to read that, we need to get you signed up so we can send you on.'"

"Next step be out in the sugar cane field." (Emlen) "I never cut sugar cane, but I willing to learn. They said we could have a rest day our first day there, but I started out the first day to familiar myself. I was really enthused being down there and what really hyped me up the most was I was going to be making four sixty-nine an hour, and I felt like I could make enough money to come back to Mississippi and work in a barber hairstyle, because I had gone to school for it and it wouldn't have taken that much for me to get the equipment I needed. They put you on a row, gave you some kneepads and all that fear gear that they wear, and told you to cut the cane. They got a guy that walks in a field, which they call a field walker. He showed us one time how to cut the cane and stack it: say cut it at the bottom, cut it at the top, fold it in your arms and lay it down.' After that, if you cut it too high, he would call you back."

"We pick it up from the Jamaicans." (Thomas) "What they did, we did. When we cut one sugar cane, they cut about eight. When we behind, they way up the field. I was studying them a little from the bus when we going to the field, but once I get out there I see I never be able to catch up to them. We'd start out at the same time in the morning and after twenty minutes they would be about three or four car lengths ahead. They were swift with their knives. They could take them and throw them across their legs real quick, sharpening them up. I don't know if they trained to do or just born to do. They looked like they had been trained for about five years before they even went out there to cut."

"Some of those stalks, it's like cutting down a miniature tree." (Emlen) "Jamaicans was on both sides of us and if we got beside a guy we had talked to in the camp he would help us. We didn't know anything about sharpening the knife, but luckily the Jamaicans showed us, because one time I said to these guys, 'Hey, how come you guys hit a stalk one time and it falls over, and I hit it six or seven times?'"

"Sugar cane is endurance, you got to be a *man* to cut sugar cane, there's nothing you can play with." (William) "I was determined to take the toil, because I had picked cotton, chopped beans, picked tomatoes. I thought maybe picking cotton was the hardest thing a man could do. I found out it was not, till I cut sugar cane. But I challenged it, I had a mind to do it. If I didn't do it, how was I going to get back to Mississippi? Either I was to swim or drown. A couple days and I started getting a little endurance, then I got a blister, but I handled it, I used mind over feelings."

"Except for the mercedes and the shinguards and the file, they didn't give us no other equipment." (Oscar) "No gloves, no shoes, no boots. I had a pair of cloth shoes I had worn over on the bus and they tore up in the fields. I had to go get my dress shoes—pair of white patent leather shoes—and wear them after. Got the patent leather all nasty. I needed a pair of boots, but we weren't issued them out. I would have brought them if I had knowed, but they didn't tell us to bring what, they just said, 'Pack up your clothes and go.'"

"Jamaicans thought we were crazy." (William) "They treated us like it was their country. You know how you go to a place and you feel kind of out of place because of the way people look at you or treat you? They would say we were lazy because we couldn't cut as fast as they could. They were suspicious of us—I don't know why. We would go over to see if there was any mail, and they would say there was none, and half an hour later some other guy would go over and here he come back with mail. Only one Jamaican I came to know. He had an ace of spaces, and an ace of hearts, and an ace of clubs in his teeth. I thought his teeth was messed up till I looked at them real close. I said, 'My goodness'; I thought it was a form of religion or something. The Jamaicans and the Dominicans and the Barbarians, or whatever they call them, are nice people, but they don't believe in being pushed to the edge in their relationships. They strong as a tree; they are strong, sturdy men. Most of the American men kind of fear these Jamaicans. They don't take too much, or they don't look like they will. I never seen any of them violent, but that was the hearsay. The women like them, cause of their accent, 'What's happening, baby,' that kind of thing. They definitely come up out of a different environment. Couldn't no man beat a Jamaican cutting sugar cane, either; they all physically endured to this kind of work. They had picked up a conditioned response to cutting cane."

"Out in the field, now, you just work." (Emlen) "Come the rice truck, if you set your food down to travel to the water wagon, the vultures would have it by the time you got back, and if you hungry after that, then damn, you chew on sugar cane. By the time we get back to the camp our pants were like heavy starch. If you go out there wearing white clothes, you can't tell what color they be when you get done. You looked like a smut baby when you come out of the field. I'll tell you something I heard down there: they say you can't bury nobody in that muck land; it just spit the coffin back up, won't keep it down. One good thing, the climate was different than Mississippi. It was dew in the morning, dew everywhere, wet as it could be, you got out there cutting sugar cane and you get sticky wet, and that cool you all day."

"The worst thing was that when we came in from the field to take a shower, we had cold water." (Oscar) "Those Jamaicans were in the same place we was, but there was a wall between us. They kept us separate. The Jamaicans that didn't go to the fields from having an injury seemed like they took showers all day. And when we turned on the showers the water would run into the sleeping area. Sometimes I don't even take a shower, because it was so filthy I believed I was cleaner than the shower. It was nasty there. It wasn't no cool place. It was nasty now."

"At night everybody be so bushed." (William) "I take a shower, get into bed and don't get up no more. Jamaicans be around playing radios, making food, drinking beer. Sometime I be too tired to eat. Where you go to sleep, you just in the open. Anybody can come through. They just walk in and walk out. It was just like an open house. Nothing was locked up. Wasn't no doors or curtains, don't have no privacy. I tried moving from upstairs to downstairs, downstairs to upstairs, it still the same."

"The social life around us seemed like it was mostly farmers selling rabbits or catching fish." (Oscar) "Some people would buy from them sometimes, but I never did. There were a lot of women. They would wear miniskirts. I met one one time and she wanted twenty dollars for some prostitution. I went as far as going to her bedroom and manipulating her a bit, but I didn't want to spend any more time with her than I did, because I needed my money to get home. Only thing I bought the whole time was some oranges. Peddlers come through selling oranges. I bought maybe five or six one time for a dollar and late at night when I wake up and can't get back to sleep I would eat some of them. There be men up shooting dice and playing cards, the men that know they aren't going to the fields the next day. Fall back asleep, then that dude come through in the morning batting on the beds with a stick or something, I don't know what he had; I never was awake to see him. He saying, 'Get up, get up, time to go.'"

"The only other thing there was about it, the food was no good." (William) "It was not a palate of American style; it was rebellious to the system in swallowing and everything. In Mississippi they told us we would be eating chicken and everything such as that. Come to find out they means beans and some type of ham hocks and turkey wings and rice. It wasn't decent at all. To get your food just go through a line like you was in prison, they dipping into the pot, throw something on your plate, throw something else, and you go ahead on. We was eating the food until one Jamaican said the meat was cats; that's why they don't have no cats about in Jamaica."

"After the eight-day training period was over was when I found out that they did take a measurement of how much you cut, and they did measure a certain length off, and you had a certain amount of time to cut that amount, and if you didn't cut that they would send you back to the bus." (Oscar) "We knew the first day, though, something was wrong, because we was wondering why they give us these slips with how much on it we cut if they paying us by the hour? About three or four days after we had been there, they started talking about some piece work. I didn't know nothing about some piece work. I never heard that. I thought it was like a job chopping cotton, where you go out in the field and you work all day, cut some weeds, nobody bothers you. They said it was going to be nasty, but they didn't say nothing about no piece work. I started getting my first check, the check look mighty fine in my hand, then I see it only for sixty-two dollars, and that was after I was there about twelve days. Go to the man, he explain what the difference is, he say it written down there in the contract. He say, 'Look at that paper, see what it say,' but I'm a little slow on reading. My last check was thirteen dollars. They took out for the transportation and their lousy food."

"My hand swole up where I couldn't even make a fist." (Emlen) "The man in charge at the camp asked me did I have twenty-five dollars and I said no, and he said if I didn't have twenty-five dollars I couldn't go to the doctor. And I told him if I couldn't go to the doctor, I couldn't go to the field. And that was when I was fired. Around that time the super come in one morning about three-thirty with a list of guys that had missed more than three days of the fields, and he went to their bunks and shook them up and said, 'Hey, you got to go.' The guys that were fired were slipping off to the orange groves. They said it was more money than sugar cane and easier too. There was a bus that would come by the store nearby to the camp; one of the first guys to get fired, he was standing on the corner and he heard people talking about it, so he ran back and got some brothers, and they went ahead and jumped on the bus. The super didn't know those guys were still sleeping in the dorms—they would leave early in the morning to catch the bus to the grove and stayed away all day, so by then they could come in. On a day off, a lot of us got together and went out into the orange groves to make some money to celebrate the new year. When we got back to the sugar cane camp the sun was just going down. The super had collected all our gear and he told us that if we weren't gone by the next day he was going to lock us in the building. Now I *know* I don't want to get locked in no building that far away from home, so we got our stuff—there were eight of us—and walked out the camp to the road, where we met this lady from Yazoo City who had just got an apartment and knew the manager and talked to him, and he told us that if we could get up forty-five dollars a week, we could rent this two-room apartment, so with the money that we had made to celebrate New Year's, we put it all together, the eight of us, and used it to get a place to live. We didn't have any lights, no gas, no hot water. The money we made in the grove on the days to come we put together, so much a day, to buy candles and something to eat. I stayed a month and a half. Wasn't really making enough money in the grove to get out, because some days we couldn't go; either the bus was broke down or it was raining. The days that we didn't go out to the orange groves we would go looking for work. We didn't get any. We got some promises. We tried a packing house for fruit, tried some stores in Belle Glade. We used to go out three and four in a group. The lady from Yazoo City started cooking short order meals for us; she gave us credit until we made money in the orange groves. Seven of us stayed there a month, and then we just started leaving one by one, because we were calling our families to send us money, or send us a ticket. When I took off, I left five guys down there. My cousin was there with me—he played poker with what he made in the groves to get money to get back and he lost it—which I hated to leave him down there, but I stayed as long as I could. The sugar companies tried to paint it like we were lazy, and I said, 'Would you call a man lazy that travels this far from home to find work?'"

"I left on a Friday with my cousin." (Thomas) "Left walking. Left Pahokee and went to Palm Beach. Caught a ride and ended up that night in Tampa sleeping in the underpass. Next day some dudes in a van took us to Wildwood, Florida. We left out of there the next morning, still coming toward Mississippi. Got another ride and made it to this church and some people gave us nineteen dollars for a ticket on the bus to Columbus, Georgia. Church in Georgia gave us money to ride home."

"A kingdom divided against itself will fall and that's what

happened." (Oscar) "We didn't get a chance to collaborate. You never get to meet the same man every day, so you can't find out how to cut sugar cane. If we could have been together, we could have coached ourselves, like a football team. When we found out we were not getting paid by the hour, we were dismayed. It really took my spirit. Everybody decided they weren't going to work no more, and that's when they put us out. It came from upstairs to get rid of us—wasn't the decision of no one person. I took my money then and bought a chicken and put it on a barbecue grill, instead of a stove, to save money. One last meal before I figured out how I was going to get home."

By 1983, approximately six thousand Haitians had settled in Belle Glade, whose population before that had been seventeen thousand. Most were from a part of Haiti that resembled Belle Glade; it is called Leogane and is the only part of Haiti without mountains. Haitians harvest the sugar cane crop in the Dominican Republic; during 1980 thousands of Haitians throughout Florida applied for jobs as cutters.

One was a young man who had arrived in Florida during the June of 1980 after spending fourteen days in a small boat adrift with twenty-three other people. In Haiti, where he was a fisherman, he belonged to a class called the unfortunates. He came to America to find a means of supporting his wife and child, as well as his mother, his father, and his grandmother. Federal immigration authorities detained him for twenty-two days in Miami, then released him in care of someone from his home town who was living in Belle Glade. That fall he had work as a cane cutter, and it turned out he was particularly good at it and had no trouble making the task. One morning after he had been working about a month, a Haitian man in his crew objected to the task he was given—the man said it was not possible to cut the length of cane in the time he had. At some point during the discussion the supervisor ran to his car. The cutter thought the supervisor had gone for a gun, so he picked up his cane knife and held it at his side. He was the only cutter who did this. All eighteen Haitians in the crew were taken then to the office of the mill, where the crew leader told a superior he had been threatened by everyone in the crew. All of them were fired. The young man went then to the state employment office, where he was told that nothing could be done for him. "If you were fired, you were fired completely," they said. The following season he applied for work cutting sugar cane. He was asked by the recruiters if he had ever cut cane in Florida. When he said that he had, they looked his name up in a book and told him that he would not be hired by any company that year.

Another Haitian cutter reached Miami in 1981 after twelve days aboard a boat with one hundred and seventy-seven others. His first fifteen months in America he spent in detention centers in Florida, Texas, and Puerto Rico and was then flown to Miami and discharged with no money. A cousin living in Belle Glade met him at the airport. He lasted thirty days as a cutter, during which ten of the fifteen Haitians in his crew were fired. He lost his job for cutting too slowly. His field boss told him that he was finished cutting cane. "When you are fired, you are fired forever," the boss said.

Thirty-eight hundred Haitians had been hired, seventeen

hundred started the season, ninety-eight finished. Growers claimed the Haitians would work well one day and not the next. A number of Haitians were injured or fell sick and discovered when they returned to the fields that they no longer had jobs. Most simply failed the productivity test, which they claimed had never been explained to them, and were gone after the eleventh day. The following year, those who reapplied stood in line, gave their names to the recruiters, watched them consult the industry's books, then heard them say no work awaited them that year in sugar cane. Many of those who had not shown up at the start of the previous season had never received word from the state employment agencies that they had been given the jobs. When they reapplied they discovered that their names were also part of the industry's records and heard the same answer. The blacklist discouraged the Haitians from working in sugar cane and they did not return.

What had happened to the Mississippians and to the Haitians became the occasion for "Job Rights of Domestic Workers: The Florida Sugar Cane Industry," prepared by the Subcommittee on Labor Standards, a part of the House of Representatives Committee on Education and Labor. During the first half of 1983, the Subcommittee staff held interviews, read documents, went three times to Belle Glade, where the Subcommittee conducted a hearing in April, and published its findings in July. They conclude that a person hoping to succeed as a cutter faces an obstacle in the form of the expectation that after eight days of practice he will be able to account for a ton of cane an hour, the amount on which the piece rate is based and the standard set by the West Indians, three-quarters of whom, the Subcommittee determined, have experience of the task. By means of a statistical sample, the Subcommittee figured that fewer than one in ten of the Haitians had come close to cutting a ton an hour (the best managed eighteen hundred pounds, ninety per cent), which led them to conclude that the standard was unreasonable. From the text: "Clearly a piece rate productivity standard that was achieved by less than 10 percent of the workforce after the eleven-day training and trial period violates the Department of Labor's policy that employers should set 'a reasonable rate of production required of a worker in order to continue on the job.'" At the hearing, the representative of the Florida Fruit and Vegetable Association said, "Our industrial society considers a piece rate system 'fair' if sixty-five percent to seventy-five percent of the workers can earn the minimum while working by the piece rate." He then claimed that ninety-five per cent of the West Indians manage to achieve the standard after eight days. How they do it the Subcommittee explains under the heading "Why Foreign Workers Are More Productive":

> The "unique and awesome form of management power" that sugar cane growers exert over their foreign workers provides a supermotivated work-force. As a vice president of U.S. Sugar once said, "If I had a remedy comparable to breaching"—that is, firing and deporting—"an unsatisfactory worker which I could apply to the American worker, they'd work harder too."

Additional obstacles the Subcommittee identifies are the blacklist, arbitrary firings, and "a clear preference for foreign workers" who "can be summarily dismissed and sent home, never to return to the United States for the slightest infraction or sign of organized protest over wages and working conditions." They find also that by providing an endless supply of West Indian cutters, the H-2 program protects the sugar cane industry from competition which might cause it to raise wages, improve working conditions, adopt attainable standards of production, and concern itself with safety, and that this amounts to a "hidden subsidy of considerable magnitude." Moreover, they find that the attitude toward improving the opportunities of domestic cutters on the part of the Department of Labor, which ought to interest itself in such things, is "near indifference, apathy, and disdain." The Department of Labor placed in control of the H-2 program a middling official in Atlanta who, in reviewing the lawfulness of the industry's practices regarding the hiring of domestic workers, relied exclusively on the Florida Fruit and Vegetable Association for information and never spoke to a cutter who had been blacklisted or challenged a single firing. Furthermore, the Subcommittee finds that the Department of Labor's failure to protect the employment rights of the Haitians "has had a devastating effect" on their community in Belle Glade.

In treating the experiences of the Mississippians the Subcommittee concludes that the recruiter who visited Mississippi had not properly explained the piece rate system and had allowed the Mississippians to believe they would be paid by the hour, or that the piece rate system would be based on a minimum requirement they would likely surpass, which "was hardly in keeping with the reality of the situation." The portion of the contract the Mississippians signed that deals with the manner of payment says, "The employer agrees to pay wages to the worker at not less than $4.69 per hour. Where the prevailing rate in the area for the work performed is higher, the higher rate shall be paid. Piece rates shall be designed to produce hourly earnings at least equivalent to the applicable hourly rates indicated in the Article, and in no event shall the worker be paid less than such hourly rate."

From the text of the report: "The omission of any information under the headings 'Piece Rate' or 'Estimated Hourly Wage' reinforces the workers' contention that they were misled into believing that they would receive $4.69 per hour, irrespective of a piece rate requirement."

When the Subcommittee visited Belle Glade for the hearing they found three of the Mississippians. Two were sharing a room without electricity in a boarding house the writer of the report described as "filthy," and one was living in an abandoned bus. The report ends with a deposition taken from Mose Rhodes, who said the recruiter had promised him at least four sixty-nine an hour, as well as free room, and board at five twenty-five a day. He said the recruiter told him the cutters would receive raises for working hard. The recruiter also explained that the work was dirty and difficult and showed them the cane knife and the hand- and shin-guards cutters wear. Rhodes was given a piece of paper which said on the top "Summary of Employment Conditions Specified on Job Order." The paper noted that his employer would be the Florida Fruit and Vegetable Association, that his period of employment was to last until April 1983, that his hourly wage would be four sixty-nine, and that the task to be performed was to "cut sugar cane as near the base as possible on assigned rows, cut the top from cane and place cane in pile row." Rhodes and nine others were boarded at Streamline, the Osceola camp in Pahokee. He went to work the first day, which was Sunday, because he was anxious to get started. He was put at the head of a row and told by a foreman to cut it. No one explained to him how to do it. By the time he had been given a row the Jamaicans were far enough along in their rows that he couldn't see how they were doing it. At the close of the day he had cut about one-half of his task. When he got back into camp and was given his time sheet he learned from talking to the Jamaicans that he would be paid for his partial accomplishment of the task, and not the hours he had worked. The highest price earned that day by any of the Mississippi workers was eleven dollars. Row prices were between thirty and forty-four dollars, which means that no one cut as much as half a row. The rest of the week Rhodes cut half a day. Work was then considered completed by the supervisors; when the Jamaicans finished their rows, they were assigned the Mississippians' rows, so the latter made no money. Rhodes always cut a row next to a Jamaican, so that the Jamaican quickly got ahead, which meant that Rhodes had the extra difficulty of the pile row against him. On the ninth day at the task Rhodes was told by the supervisor that the following day he would be judged to see if he was up to speed, and that if he wasn't he would be fired. That day he and the other Mississippians were awakened at four by the supervisor who told them they no longer worked for the company. Rhodes was told that someone had reported to the supervisor that he and the nine other men from Mississippi in the barracks had missed work to pick oranges. Rhodes said he hadn't but was fired anyway. The supervisor said that since the men no longer worked for the company they would get no food for that day, and would have to leave the camp by nightfall. If they were not out, the supervisor said, he would lock the barracks and call the sheriff. The nine went into town and found a room and, since they had no money, joined an orange-picking crew being assembled at the ramp. When they returned to Osceola for their pay, Rhodes got no money, only a check stub explaining the deductions from his wages. For his ten days' work cutting cane he had made ninety-three dollars and two cents. At the time he was interviewed, Rhodes was living in Belle Glade, picking oranges three days a week for fifteen dollars a day and trying to raise the money to get back to Mississippi. He was to be evicted in three days from his room because he was behind in his rent. While he was in Florida his children were living with his mother-in-law in Mississippi. (His wife was dead.) The deposition concludes, "I still need a job, and I would be willing to cut cane for the $4.69 an hour that I was originally promised."

44

Cutters occasionally come in from the cane fields and lie down and never get up. They get into arguments in town and are shot. They die in car accidents. As far as I know a West Indian has never died in the cane fields.

The last man I know of to die in a cane camp died in his sleep at South Shore Camp in the December of 1987. The others rose and got ready for work and saw him lying on his bed. His body was returned to Jamaica. South Shore belongs to U.S. Sugar. A collection was taken up among the company's camps for his widow. There was some unpleasantness about this. Men at one camp gave seven hundred dollars and those at another gave three hundred. The supervisors said to the men who had given three hundred that this was not sufficient and that they must give more. It is not that the cutters were ungenerous or unwilling to help, but they felt it was the responsibility of the company to assist the widow.

When a man dies on the contract an official from the Ministry of Labor finds his widow (or his mother or his girlfriend) and breaks the news. Usually they arrive two or three days after the event. The companies return the bodies to Montego Bay or to Kingston; the families must stand any further expense for transportation, and if they can't or won't, the men are buried in Florida.

Sometimes tractor drivers fall asleep at the wheel and turn the tractor into the canal. This happens once or twice a year to each company. Men bring their friends into the office and say they know how to drive and either they do or they don't, or they are hopped up or hung over and tired or still drunk from the night before. This happens most often on Saturday or Sunday mornings. The drivers almost always survive.

One year a truck carrying cutters to the fields turned over and two were killed. This was reported at some length in the Florida papers. The only death I know of related to sugar cane that received widespread attention over a period of time was not that of a cutter, but of a college girl who was assisting pickets at the Talisman Sugar Company, in 1972, and in the middle of the night was struck accidentally by a cane truck entering the mill. Stories about it appeared in papers throughout Florida over several weeks. No witness ever suggested that her death was not accidental—that is, no one ever thought that the growers had intended harm towards the strikers. Nor was there anything sensational about the circumstances of the accident. Nor had any kind of celebrity surrounded the girl. What accounted for the continuing interest was the ghoulish and inexplicable conclusion drawn by the industry and the Florida Highway Patrol to fit the events of that night.

The name of the young woman killed was Nan Freeman. She died early in the morning of January 25, 1972. She was from Massachusetts and she was eighteen years old. She had received a number of letters from colleges offering full scholarships but was interested only in schools that provided opportunities for independent study. She selected the New College in Sarasota and her parents drove her to Florida in the September of 1971. Over the course of the fall she sent them many letters written in her small hand which her father said made notebooks of postcards. She worked for no pay at a nursery for black families as well as at a school for retarded children. During Thanksgiving vacation she had a chance to visit a halfway house in North Carolina. It was fourteen hours by bus from the campus. She returned to school having written two hundred pages on prisons and prison reform. Through a course at college she and other students had become involved with the United Farm Workers and had volunteered to assist the strikers at the mill. The strike included approximately two hundred of Talisman's employees, the majority of whom drove trucks. Most of the drivers were Cubans from the Little Havana section of Miami, sixty miles southeast from the mill. They were working twelve hours a day, with no days off, and had requested shorter hours and breaks for meals, and were fired. An official of the United Farm Workers had been in the area on other business and had driven past the mill and noticed the drivers' protest and had given it the support of the Union. Talisman hired other drivers.

The pickets were taking turns flagging them down at the entrance to the mill and handing out leaflets and talking to any who stopped.

The road to the mill runs beside a canal and joins State Road 27 at an angle of ninety degrees. Each side of it fans out slightly to make the turn less abrupt. The trailer of a truck turning too sharply into the mill would strike a guard rail beside the canal. On the night Nan Freeman was killed two deputies from the Palm Beach County Sheriff's Department sat in a car across the canal from the entrance to the mill—that is to say, about a hundred feet or less from the gate. It happened to be a night of a heavy fog. Around three-thirty in the morning four people—Nan Freeman; José Romero, an organizer for the Union; William Nogues, a driver on strike; and Pam Albright, a student at the college—stood beside the guard rail and watched a truck approach through the fog. One of them waved to the driver, who brought his truck to a stop on the mill road. Romero climbed up on the cab and spoke to him through the passenger's window. The driver was sympathetic and gave Romero the impression he would consider parking his truck and joining the picket line. While they were talking, the headlights of a second truck appeared about three hundred feet up the road and its driver sounded his horn to move the first truck on to the mill. Romero jumped down off the cab and the truck started up. Nogues was sitting on the guard rail, about five feet from the others and closer to the highway, when the second truck turned sharply onto the mill road. Nan Freeman, Pam Albright, and José Romero were standing on the road talking about the small victory with the driver. The back wheel of the trailer pinned Nan Freeman against the guard rail, then flung her forward in a somersault onto the road. The truck continued toward the mill; no one believed the driver was aware of what had happened. José Romero pulled Nan onto the grass behind the guard rail, then ran immediately to the deputies and asked them to call an ambulance because one of the pickets had just been run over. The deputies came to see what had happened. They found Pam Albright kneeling beside Nan Freeman, who was not conscious. Blood flowed from her nose and from her mouth. One of the deputies said, "You kids had no business being here." Pam Albright remembers that at a certain moment, Nan let out a deep breath, like a sigh, and one of the deputies said, "She's gone home."

On the night that her daughter died, Mrs. Freeman slept fitfully. "I heard a voice," she says, "and it's very strange and I swear it's true—my daughter called me Mama—and I heard her, and I got up and went into her room and I said 'How stupid, she's away at college,' then the phone rang and Marshall Barry, her teacher, called and said there's been an accident and she was hurt. No one called me from Florida to tell me, not the police, nobody ever; they never even returned her effects. If it wasn't for our town police who called Florida we never would have known anything, because I called the people in Florida and they got on the phone and said we got no information. Marshall gave me a number where they're supposed to bring her to a hospital; I called them, they said nobody was there. When I finally heard she was dead, I was so upset that I sat down and wrote a poem, instead of screaming out my feelings."

. . .

Reading *A History of the Florida Sugar Industry*, by George H. Salley, published in 1984 and distributed by the Sugar Cane League, I came across these sentences:

> Beginning with Okeelanta, most of the mills were unionized without serious opposition or disruption. However, Cesar Chavez has made several attempts to unionize the agricultural employees, so far unsuccessfully. On one of these occasions helping to picket the Talisman mill were students from the ultra-liberal New College in Sarasota, one of whom, found dead at the entrance to the mill, the union organizers claimed had been run over by a truckload of sugarcane entering the plant. Fortunately, a deputy sheriff was on duty at the gate at the time and investigation by the Florida Highway Patrol disclosed that the girl had died elsewhere and was dead when brought to Talisman.

The Florida Highway Patrol investigation of Nan Freeman's death is filed according to the designation FHP-772-6-2 and has become a public document. It contains a number of items, including statements by witnesses, the transcript of a hearing held in West Palm Beach at which Pam Albright told what she knew; an autopsy report; drawings of the accident scene; a letter from Dr. Joseph H. Davis, the Dade County Medical Examiner; and a case summary of sixteen pages written by G. L. McLain, the trooper who conducted the investigation. McLain arrived at the entrance of the mill two hours after the accident. One of the deputies showed him where the body had been found and told him that the truck responsible had gone on to the mill before the deputies had been made aware of what had happened. From the log at the mill it was possible to tell immediately what two trucks had been described by the deputy. The trucks were numbered 166 and 179. Their drivers had left the mill at five, when their shift had ended. At eight o'clock that morning McLain took a statement from José Romero. That afternoon he attended Nan Freeman's autopsy, performed against the wishes and religious beliefs of her family, at which it was determined that she died of internal injuries resulting from having had her chest and her abdomen crushed. The day passed. McLain went here and there. He mentions no attempt to reach the drivers of the trucks. That evening at six-fifty-five, fifteen and a half hours after the accident, the Highway Patrol station in Pahokee received a call from one of the drivers who said that he had heard about the accident and had been told by the company that the Highway Patrol wanted to talk to him and that he was returning to the mill and would call when he arrived. McLain went to the mill with a trooper named Pursell and interviewed the drivers. The troopers talked first to the driver of truck 179, the one who had spoken to José Romero. The story he told did not agree with the one provided by Romero. The driver told the troopers he had not stopped at the entrance to the mill, only slowed to change gears, and that while he did a Mexican male jumped up on the passenger's side of his cab. He said that although he often saw girls among the pickets at the entrance to the mill, none was there on that occasion.

The troopers then spoke to the driver of truck 166. His story did not agree in any detail with the one told by Romero, although it was consistent with the one told by the other driver. He said that he had been following truck 179 into the mill at a distance of about five hundred feet and that truck 179 had not stopped at the entrance. Furthermore, he said that he had not sounded his horn to move 179 on to the mill.

McLain writes that the drivers were interviewed outside each others' presence and that the first driver was "very co-operative" and that the second told a story that "seemed to corroborate the story of the other driver." That they had rehearsed it, to protect either themselves or the company from liability (and either on their own or under instructions from the company), is a possibility he does not raise.

When McLain and Pursell had finished their interviews, the drivers went back to work. Leaving the mill, the troopers stopped to question a picket they thought had been present at the time of the accident. The man told them he had been at the scene but had been asleep at the time in his car. McLain considers this man to be of no consequence to his investigation and neither records his name nor talks to him again. He is one of only three men in the entire homicide report, which is eighty-two pages, not to be identified by name, the other two being the drivers of trucks 166 and 179.

McLain begins his discussion of the next day's events by noting the arrival at three minutes after ten that morning of a call from an attorney for the Union saying that witnesses to the accident are at the picket line and can be interviewed there. He excludes from his summary the information that two-and-a-half hours earlier, at seven-twenty-five, he took a statement from Deputy Purvis, one of the two deputies on duty at the mill when the accident took place, in which Purvis told him (as had Romero) that a cane truck pulled into the entrance of the mill and stopped, and that in about a minute a second truck appeared up the highway and blew his horn to move the first truck on to the mill.

Later that day McLain received a written statement from C. W. Lowell, the second deputy, which he also fails to note. Deputy Lowell reported (as had Romero and Deputy Purvis) that he saw a cane truck approach from the north, enter the mill, stop and talk to the pickets (a detail Romero had mentioned but not Deputy Purvis) and that a second truck appeared on the highway and that as this truck drew closer to the gates its driver sounded his horn to move the first truck on to the mill.

Nowhere in his report does McLain acknowledge the deputies' and Romero's contradiction of the drivers' story. To do so would establish the truthfulness of Romero's account, and McLain's conclusion—that Nan Freeman was killed somewhere else and her body placed at the gates of the mill by the strikers—would then be insupportable.

That night Pursell interviewed the drivers for the final time. McLain discloses nothing of what was said, only that the drivers had nothing to add.

During February the Palm Beach *Times* ran an article regarding Nan Freeman's death under the headline "Coed Hit by Someone Else." The article says that William Pawley, the owner of Talisman, told reporters in Miami, where he lived, that he believed the Highway Patrol investigation into Nan Freeman's death would find that his company was blameless.

> Pawley said he believes that Nan Freeman, 18, a student at Sarasota's New College, may have been struck by a vehicle on U.S. Highway 27, then moved by other picketers to the gateway of the Talisman Sugar Mill, 15 miles south of South Bay.
>
> Striking Mexican, Cuban, white and black sugar-mill workers told the Florida Highway Patrol the morning of the accident that a sugar truck accidentally struck the girl as it pulled through the gates. . . .
>
> "This girl was not run over by a Talisman truck and we feel confident that no Talisman truck struck her . . . that she was a victim of Route 27," Pawley said. . . .
>
> The former ambassador said a striker's identification of a Talisman truck by the truck number proved to be wrong. He said a sheriff's investigation indicated that the truck had not been out of the garage for a week.

The Highway Patrol would neither confirm nor deny Pawley's remarks. A spokesman for the Sheriff's Department told the *Times* that the investigation Pawley referred to as having discovered that the Talisman truck blamed for the accident had not been out of the garage for a week had never taken place.

In March, the Florida Highway Patrol concluded its investigation, finding exactly what Pawley had predicted in February that it would. In his closing, McLain wrote, "It is the opinion of this investigator that the loaded cane truck did not hit this girl and that she was perhaps run over by another vehicle. The injuries appear to this investigator to have come from a lighter vehicle, such as a car or perhaps a small van type vehicle."

The report ends:

> It is the opinion of this investigator that this case should remain open as to the pending information concerning the name of the driver and type vehicle involved in this accident. Therefore, not allowing this report to become a matter of public record until this case can be officially closed and any possible charges placed against anyone who may have committed a criminal act.

McLain's report was reviewed for Marvin Mounts, the Palm Beach County Solicitor, by Dr. Joseph H. Davis, the medical examiner of Dade County. Dr. Davis's reply suggests an awkward situation. One assumes he had been asked to review the report in the expectation that he would find in it reason to support its conclusion. Instead he wrote,

> After review of the above documents and photographs, it seems apparent that independent witnesses not capable of acting in collusion, including proponents of the sugar mill strike, police, and drivers, can place two tractor trailers at the inter-

> section, one following the other, on or about the time of the incident. Minor discrepancies as to whether or not the first vehicle came to a complete halt are present but do not seem to detract from the overall aspects. It seems unlikely that the first vehicle collided with the guard rail but it could possibly have come close. According to Dr. Ramos [who performed the autopsy] "the victim did not have road dirt on her clothing to indicate that she was crushed against the ground. The pattern of injuries, including the fractures of the left forearm, would seem to indicate that she could have been partially crushed between the trailer and the guard rail."

Nan Freeman's parents sued Talisman. It took them some time to find a lawyer. Several refused them. One, they said, accepted the case, let almost a year pass, then told them he couldn't do anything with it. The lawyer they finally engaged said they were taking a gamble suing a sugar company in south Florida. Talisman's lawyers sought a settlement. Mrs. Freeman had hoped to press the case. In the end, she and her husband decided that the trips to Florida for the trial, the wait for the case to be heard and the delays the company would seek, the difficulty of facing a public revival of the events, and the money a trial would cost were more than they were willing to endure, and agreed to the settlement.

Each year on the anniversary of their daughter's death, the Freemans visit the gates of the Talisman mill. On the occasion of their first trip, in 1974 (they could not bring themselves to go in 1973), the company was having labor problems and had posted at the entrance guards who had guns. While the Freemans and others with them said their prayers, the guards looked on. Mrs. Freeman thinks the guards might have had the courtesy to turn the other way, instead of facing them with guns, but they didn't.

45

When the cutters depart the bus for the fields in the morning the stars are out. On the horizon in the east is a band of orange as straight and precise as the inlay on a piece of furniture. They leave the bus by the exits at the front and the back, holding the cutlass before them in order to keep their eyes on the blade. Some line up at the closest row, others race ahead, searching. Fog blankets the fields and the headlands, the road ahead and behind, and the ditches; it looks like mist rising from the surface of a lake; it looks as if the fields are steaming. It is too early for birds. The only sounds are the ones the cutters make: shouts on meeting the cold, the metallic click of their shinguards as they walk, the muffled thud of the blade at work. By the time the pusher reads the row price from a slip of paper held up to the headlights of the bus, and calls out the figure, the cutters are already at work. Sweat rises from their shoulders and backs like vapor off the back of a horse. The pusher shouts, "Cut that stubble, pile that cane good. Too much stubble. Get that stubble, man. Do good work. Cut that top, man. It get you warm in a minute. Yeah, yeah, yeah." As they move down the rows, they first become shadows, then disappear into the mist.

AUTHOR'S NOTE

I have not been able to include in the text the names of all the people to whom I am grateful for help. Among them are the following:

In Florida: Marshall Barry, Frank O'Loughlin, Judith Petersen, Jerrell H. Shofner, Wayne Smith, Rob Williams.

In Washington: Doug Bowers, Mary Ronan, Martin Tolchin.

At *The New Yorker*: Nancy Boensch, Patrick Crow, Bruce Diones, Deborah Garrison, Ann Goldstein, Adam Gopnik, Eleanor Gould, Martha Kaplan, Charles McGrath, Sheila McGrath, Ben Narvaez, William Shawn, Josselyn Simpson, Helen Stark, Pat Strachan, Natasha Turi.

At Alfred A. Knopf: Paul Bogaards, Janice Goldklang, Ann Kraybill, Nicholas Latimer, William Loverd, Rahna Rizzuto.

In Mississippi: Johnnie E. Walls.

In New York: Stephanie Black, Deborah Karl, Roger Kimball, Susan Schorr.

I would like in particular to acknowledge the importance to me of the contributions made by:

Charlotte Sibley, at the Florida Rural Legal Services.
Edward Tuddenham, of the Migrant Legal Action Program.
The John Simon Guggenheim Memorial Foundation.
Ann Close and A. S. Mehta, of Alfred A. Knopf.
Robert Gottlieb, of *The New Yorker.*
Andrew Wylie.
William Maxwell.

ABOUT THE AUTHOR

Alec Wilkinson is the author of *Midnights: A Year with the Wellfleet Police* and *Moonshine: A Life in Pursuit of White Liquor.* He lives with his wife in New York City and since 1980 has been a writer on the staff of *The New Yorker.*